Formative assessment in second language learning: a systematic review and an annotated bibliography

Written by Skevi Vassiliou,
Salomi Papadima-Sophocleous,
and Christina Nicole Giannikas

Published by Research-publishing.net, a not-for-profit association
Voillans, France, info@research-publishing.net

© 2022 by Authors

Formative assessment in second language learning: a systematic review and an annotated bibliography
Written by Skevi Vassiliou, Salomi Papadima-Sophocleous, and Christina Nicole Giannikas

Publication date: 2022/11/21

Rights: this book is published under the Attribution-NonCommercial-NoDerivatives International (CC BY-NC-ND) licence. Under this licence, the book is freely available online (https://doi.org/10.14705/rpnet.2022.60.9782383720133) for anybody to read, download, copy, and redistribute provided that the authors and publisher are properly cited. Commercial use and derivative works are, however, not permitted.

Disclaimer: Research-publishing.net does not take any responsibility for the content of the pages written by the authors of this book. The authors have recognised that the work described was not published before, or that it was not under consideration for publication elsewhere. While the information in this book is believed to be true and accurate on the date of its going to press, neither the editorial team nor the publisher can accept any legal responsibility for any errors or omissions. The publisher makes no warranty, expressed or implied, with respect to the material contained herein. While Research-publishing.net is committed to publishing works of integrity, the words are the authors' alone.

Trademark notice: product or corporate names may be trademarks or registered trademarks, and are used only for identification and explanation without intent to infringe.

Copyrighted material: every effort has been made to trace copyright holders and to obtain their permission for the use of copyrighted material in this book. In the event of errors or omissions, please notify the publisher of any corrections that will need to be incorporated in future editions of this book.

Typeset by Research-publishing.net
Cover design and photo by © Raphaël Savina (raphael@savina.net)

ISBN13: 978-2-38372-013-3 (Ebook, PDF, colour)
ISBN13: 978-2-38372-014-0 (Ebook, EPUB, colour)
ISBN13: 978-2-38372-012-6 (Paperback - Print on demand, black and white)
Print on demand technology is a high-quality, innovative and ecological printing method; with which the book is never 'out of stock' or 'out of print'.

British Library Cataloguing-in-Publication Data.
A cataloguing record for this book is available from the British Library.

Legal deposit, France: Bibliothèque Nationale de France - Dépôt légal: 2022 novembre.

Table of contents

Notes on contributors v
Acknowledgements ix
List of abbreviations and acronyms xi

Foreword xv

Introduction 1

Part 1. Formative assessment in review 7

1.1.	*Formative assessment*	*7*
1.2.	*Formative assessment in language learning*	*12*
1.3.	*Systematic Review (SR)*	*18*
1.4.	*Annotated Bibliography (AB)*	*19*
1.5.	*Why combine SR and AB?*	*19*

Part 2. A systematic review of formative assessment in language learning 29

2.1.	*Introduction*	*29*
2.2.	*Methodology*	*31*
2.3.	*Results*	*38*
2.4.	*Discussion*	*52*
2.5.	*Limitations*	*64*
2.6.	*Conclusions*	*65*

Table of contents

Part 3. An annotated bibliography in formative assessment in language learning   77

3.1.   *Introduction*   *77*
3.2.   *Methodology*   *78*
3.3.   *Annotated bibliography entries*   *81*

Conclusions   157

Notes on contributors

Authors

Skevi Vassiliou is a Greek language instructor and researcher. She is a PhD candidate in Education (curriculum and instruction) at Saint Louis University (US). She holds an MA in computer assisted language learning from Cyprus University of Technology, an MA in Education from Saint Louis (US), and a BA in Greek language and literature from Aristotle University of Thessaloniki. Her research interests include formative assessment in L2 teaching and learning, technology applications for formative assessment second language learning purposes, and teaching methodologies in second language teaching and learning.

Salomi Papadima-Sophocleous (BA, GradCertEd, DipEd, MEd, MLit, PostGradDipCALL, and Dprof in applied linguistics – online English testing) was the Cyprus University of Technology (CUT) Language Centre Director and MA in computer assisted language learning Coordinator. She retired on May 31, 2021. Currently she holds a position as a researcher at the Cyprus Interaction Lab in the Department of Multimedia and Graphic Arts at CUT. Her research interests, in which she has been publishing articles and books since 1982, are mainly in language teaching (ESP, Greek, French, Italian, Turkish), computer assisted language learning, online curriculum development and evaluation, computer assisted language assessment and testing, onsite/online teacher education, and extend to biographies of Limassol multilingual/multicultural schools, and Limassol oral history. She has co-edited the *International Experiences in Language Testing and Assessment* (2013); *CALL Communities and Cultures* (2016); *Professional Development in CALL: A Selection of Papers* (2019); *ESP Teaching and Teacher Education: Current*

Notes on contributors

Theories and Practices (2019); *Tertiary Education Language Learning: A Collection of Research (2021);* and *Langues Moins Diffusées et Moins Enseignées (MoDiMEs – 2020.)* She is the editor of 17 volumes of proceedings of the Annual Oral History Symposium of the Pattichion Municipal Museum, Historical Archive and Research Centre of Limassol. She is the author of *The Private School of Foreign Language and Greek Lessons: 1920-1950, Biography of a school in Limassol* (2020). Her forthcoming book is *Saint Mary's School of Limassol (1923-2023): A multilingual and multicultural school before its time* (2023). She participated in and led a number of nationally and internationally funded projects. She was an elected member of the EUROCALL Association Executive Committee, the Association 9 SIGs' coordinator and EuroCALL's National Contact for Cyprus

Christina Giannikas, holds a PhD in the field of applied linguistics. She is an education and research consultant and founder of CG Education and Research Consultancy, an online certified tutor, EAP/ESP instructor, materials writer, editor, and co-owner of the Giannikas Foreign Language Schools. She also works in higher education where she lectures courses in applied linguistics, she is involved in research projects with international partners and is a teacher trainer for pre-service and in-service teacher education programmes in Cyprus and beyond. Over the years, Christina has collaborated with publishers, such as HarperCollins and Cambridge University Press, ELT/TESOL associations, such as QLS (Greece) and Ministries of Education (UAE, Cyprus) on a number of projects offering consultancy, research, editing, and material writing services. She specialises in the areas of early language learning, age-appropriate digital pedagogies, digital literacies, assessment, and teacher education. For the last six years, Christina has been serving as Chair of the EuroCALL Teacher Education SIG and is the EuroCALL National Contact for Greece. Some of her most recent book publications include: Papadima-Sophocleous, S., Kakoulli-Constantinou, E., and **Giannikas, C.N.** (2021), *Tertiary Education Language Learning: a collection of CALL & LSP research.* Research-publishing.net (Open Access); **Giannikas, C.N.** (2021), *Teaching Practices and Equitable Learning in Children's Language Education*; and **Giannikas, C.N.** (2022), *Transferring Language Learning and Teaching from Face-to-Face to Online Settings.*

Invited Author

Dina Tsagari is Professor in English Language Pedagogy/TESOL, in the Department of Primary and Secondary Teacher Education OsloMet – Oslo Metropolitan University, Norway. She holds a PhD in Linguistics (language testing) from Lancaster University, UK. She has previously worked for the University of Cyprus and the Greek Open University. Her research interests include language testing and assessment, teacher training, materials design and evaluation, differentiated instruction, multilingualism, distance education, and learning difficulties. She coordinates research groups, e.g. CBLA SIG – EALTA, EnA OsloMet and is involved in EU-funded and other research projects (e.g. SCALED, KIDS4ALL, NORHED, KriT, DINGLE, TRIBES, ENRICH, TALE, DysTEFL, PALM, etc). Her webpage: https://www.oslomet.no/om/ansatt/dintsa/

Reviewer

Angela Scarino is Associate Professor in Applied Linguistics and Director of the Research Centre for Languages and Cultures, in Justice and Society at the University of South Australia. Her research expertise is in languages education in linguistically and culturally diverse societies, second language learning within an intercultural orientation, second language assessment, and second language teacher education. She has been a Chief Investigator on a range of research grants. She has worked in diverse contexts beyond Australia, including Hong Kong, Singapore, Malaysia, France and New Zealand). She is an associate editor for the Modern Language Journal and a member of a number of editorial boards. Books include Intercultural Language Teaching and learning (with Tony Liddicoat, 2013 Wiley-Blackwell), Dynamic ecologies: a relational perspective on language education in the Asia-Pacific region (edited volume with Neil Murray, 2014. Springer).

Acknowledgements

We would like to thank the following people for their help and support during the production of this book.

We would like to thank Angela Scarino of the University of South Australia for the review of the book and her valuable suggestions.

We would also like to thank Dina Tsagari of Oslo Metropolitan University for her insightful foreword.

List of abbreviations and acronyms

- AaL: Assessment as Learning
- AB: Annotated Bibliography
- ACTFL: American Council on the Teaching of Foreign Languages
- AEW: Academic English Writing
- AFL: Assessment For Learning
- ANCOVA: Analysis of covariance
- APA: American Psychological Association
- AWE: Automated Writing Evaluation
- CA: Conversation Analysis
- CALAT: Computer Assisted Language Assessment and Testing
- CALL: Computer Assisted Language Learning
- CBLA: Classroom-Based Language Assessment
- CHC: Confucian Heritage Culture
- CEFR: Common European Framework of Reference
- CLIL: Content and Language Integrated Learning
- COVID-19: Coronavirus disease of 2019
- CPD: Continuing Professional Development
- CRESST: Centre for Research on Evaluation Standards, and Student Testing
- DA: Dynamic Assessment
- EAL: English as an Additional Language
- EAP: English for Academic Purposes
- EFL: English as a Foreign Language
- ELL: English Language Learners
- ELA: English Language Arts
- ELD: English Language Development
- ELFA: English Learner Formative Assessment
- ELFA: English Language Formative Assessment

Abbreviations and acronyms

- ERIC: Education Resources Information Center
- ELP: European Language Portfolio
- ESL: English as a Second Language
- ETS: Educational Testing Service
- FA: Formative Assessment
- FAoW: Formative Assessment of Writing
- FG: Focus group
- FL: Foreign Language
- GLP: Global Language Portfolio
- IBM: International Business Machines Corporation
- IELTS: International English Language Testing System
- LAL: Language Assessment Literacy
- LL: Language Learning
- LF: LinguaFolio
- LOA: Learning-Oriented Assessment
- L2: Second Language
- MA: Master of Arts
- MLA: Modern Language Association
- OPE: Open Peer Feedback
- PA: Portfolio Assessment
- PGT: Postgraduate Taught
- PhD: Doctor of Philosophy
- QMP: Question Mark Perception
- QUAL: Qualitative
- QUAN: Quantitative
- RPLE: Reference to a post-learning activity
- SA: Summative Assessment
- SPSS: Statistical Package for the Social Sciences
- SR: Systematic Review
- TEAL: Teachers of English as an Additional Language
- TESOL: Teaching English to Speakers of other Languages
- TOEIC: Test of English for International Communication
- TOEFL Test of English as a Foreign Language
- TPS: Think-Pair-Share

- VAM: Video Assessment Module
- WRM: Writing Road Map
- ZPD: Zone of Proximal Development

Foreword

Over the recent years research has focused on teachers' assessment activities as an integral part of classroom activity (Tsagari & Csépes, 2011) while research projects and reforms have been implemented in classroom assessment (Hamp-Lyons, 2016). The growing awareness of the importance of assessment activities as a central part of classroom assessment also came with the initial discussions of Formative Assessment (FA) (Black & Wiliam, 1998a, 2009). Over the years, FA, also the focus of this book, has become an emerging paradigm of its own. Other than its exciting and evolving agenda of research, FA places a great deal of and links assessment with language learning (Airasian, 2001; Black & Wiliam, 1998b, 2009; Harlen, 2012; Torrance, 2012).

Nevertheless, researchers and practitioners in the field have proposed additional terms that echo similar characteristics of FA, e.g. *classroom-based (language) assessment* (Rea-Dickins, 2008; Tsagari & Csépes, 2011; Turner, 2012), *assessment for learning* (Asghar, 2010; Blanchard, 2008; Boyle & Charles, 2010), *learning-oriented assessment* (Pryor & Crossouard, 2008; Tsagari, 2014; Turner & Purpura, 2016), *classroom evaluation* (Crooks, 1988), *diagnostic assessment* (Alderson, 2005), *dynamic assessment* (Lantolf & Poehner, 2008), *alternative assessment* (Inbar-Lourie & Donitsa-Schmidt, 2009), and *interactive assessment* (Hamp-Lyons & Tavares, 2011).

The variety of terms used to describe similar processes of classroom assessment manifests a difficulty in providing a standard definition of FA (Boyle & Charles, 2010; Turner, 2012). Nevertheless, the term 'formative assessment' was first attributed to Scriven (1967) in his attempt to make a distinction between 'formative evaluation' (evaluation taking place during the lesson) and 'summative evaluation' (evaluation taking place at the end of a unit).

Foreword

Other definitions of FA focus on the modification of instruction to improve teaching and learning, as well as on the provision of feedback (Bloom, Hastings, & Madaus, 1971; Clark, 2010; Frey & Schmidt, 2007; Hattie & Timperley, 2007; etc). Further definitions of FA focus on the purposes and strategies used in its implementation which emphasise the importance of criteria of learning and offering learners formative and constructive feedback (Ioannou & Tsagari, 2022a, 2022b), or focus on questioning and observation (Chin & Teou, 2010; Michaeloudes, 2018) or self-assessment (Bachman & Palmer, 1996) and peer-assessment (Meletiadou & Tsagari, 2022; Tsagari & Meletiadou, 2015). Other FA definitions focus on the changes needed in instruction so that teaching and learning can be improved (e.g. Assessment Reform Group, 2002; Black & Wiliam, 1998a, 2009). This is actually the foundation of FA as all assessment types undertaken should lead to change with a view to better performance.

However, the variety of terms and types of assessment used to describe processes similar to FA, or used even interchangeably with it, the different viewpoints on the origin of the term, and the different definitions of the term 'formative' has created an ambiguity in the area of FA. On the other hand, research in FA has critically expanded, and new, refreshing, and unexplored avenues have made their appearance in the field of language assessment.

For example a number of studies in both general education and FL/L2 learning show that FA is an effective teaching strategy which promotes learning and develops learners' autonomy (Black & Wiliam, 1998a; Ellery, 2008; Stiggins, 2002; Taras, 2008; Tsagari & Michaeloudes, 2012, 2013). More specifically, FA seems to have significant effects on primary education (Carless, 2005; Rea-Dickins, 2006) as well as adult education (Ioannou & Tsagari, 2022a, 2022b).

However, even though FA has proved to be effective, research has found that teachers have some difficulties in implementing FA-related practices. Research on teachers' understanding of FA (Boyle & Charles, 2010; Michaeloudes, 2018; Vogt & Tsagari, 2014) reveals that they are not always clear of what FA actually is. Tsagari (2021) found that teachers have inadequate skills and strategies to design, and implement FA practices (also in Tsagari & Vogt, 2017; Vogt, Tsagari,

& Spanoudis, 2020). Inadequate knowledge may be the reason why teachers are hesitant in using FA (Colby-Kelly & Turner, 2007) and handle FA practices in the same way as summative practices (Ayala et al., 2008). This should be investigated further as teachers' understanding and cognition affect their practices. Therefore, further research in the field of FA seems to be necessary for successful FA implementation.

Against this background, the authors of this book address timely aspects of FA for the research and teaching community in language assessment research, language teaching, and other related areas. The book is based on systematic review of theoretical and research papers in the field of FA that are presented in the discussion of the first two parts as well as in part three as annotated bibliography.

Overall, this volume, characterised by scholarly work in the evolving and expanding field of FA, will become an important resource that broadens the existing approaches undertaken to date. The volume is an important reference source and can become essential reading material for graduate students, teacher trainers, and practitioners in the field of language assessment.

Dr Dina Tsagari

Department of Primary and Secondary Teacher Education, Faculty of Education and Internationalisation OsloMet, Oslo, Norway

References

Airasian, P. W. (2001). *Classroom assessment: concepts and applications.* McGraw-Hill.

Alderson, J. C. (2005). *Diagnosing foreign language proficiency: the interface between learning and assessment.* Continuum.

Asghar, A. (2010). Reciprocal peer coaching and its use as a formative assessment strategy for first-year students. *Assessment & Evaluation in Higher Education, 35*(4), 403-417. https://doi.org/10.1080/02602930902862834

Assessment Reform Group. (2002). *Providing constructive responses to learning. Effective feedback: principles, policy and audit materials.* University of Cambridge.

Ayala, C. C., Shavelson, R. J., Ruiz-Primo, M. A., Brandon, P. R., Yin, Y., Furtak, E. M., Young, D. B., & Tomita, M. K. (2008). From formal embedded assessments to reflective lessons: the development of formative assessment studies. *Applied Measurement in Education, 21*(4), 315-334. https://doi.org/10.1080/08957340802347787

Bachman, L., & Palmer, A. (1996). *Language testing in practice.* Oxford University Press.

Black, P., & Wiliam, D. (1998a). Inside the black box: raising standards through classroom assessment. *Phi Delta Kappa, 80*(2), 123-148.

Black, P., & Wiliam, D. (1998b). Assessment and classroom learning. *Assessment in Education: Principles, Policy & Practice, 5*(1), 7-74. https://doi.org/10.1080/0969595980050102

Black, P., & Wiliam, D. (2009). Developing the theory of formative assessment. *Educational Assessment, Evaluation and Accountability, 21*(1), 5. https://doi.org/10.1007/s11092-008-9068-5

Blanchard, J. (2008). Learning awareness: constructing formative assessment in the classroom, in the school and across schools. *The Curriculum Journal, 19*(3), 137-150. https://doi.org/10.1080/09585170802357454

Bloom, B. S., Hastings, J. T., & Madaus, G. F. (1971). *Handbook on the formative and summative evaluation of student learning.* McGraw-Hill.

Boyle, W. F., & Charles, M. (2010). Leading learning through assessment for learning? *School Leadership & Management, 30*(3), 285-300. https://doi.org/10.1080/13632434.2010.485184

Carless, D. (2005). Prospects for the implementation of assessment for learning. *Assessment in Education: Principles, Policy & Practice, 12*(1), 39-54. https://doi.org/10.1080/0969594042000333904

Chin, C, & Teou, L.-Y. (2010). Formative assessment: using concept cartoon, pupils' drawings, and group discussions to tackle children's ideas about biological inheritance. *Educational Research, 44*(3), 108-115. https://doi.org/10.1080/00219266.2010.9656206

Clark, I. (2010). Formative assessment: 'there is nothing so practical as a good theory. *Australian Journal of Education, 54*(3), 341-352. https://doi.org/10.1177/000494411005400308

Colby-Kelly, C., & Turner, C. E. (2007). AFL research in the L2 classroom and evidence of usefulness: taking formative assessment to the next level. *The Canadian Modern Language Review/La Revue canadienne des langues vivantes, 64*(1), 9-38. https://doi.org/10.3138/cmlr.64.1.009

Crooks, T. J. (1988). The impact of classroom evaluation practices on students. *Review of Educational Research, 58*(4), 438-448. https://doi.org/10.3102/00346543058004438

Ellery, K. (2008). Assessment for learning: a case study using feedback effectively in an essay-style test. *Assessment & Evaluation in Higher Education, 33*(4), 421-429. https://doi.org/10.1080/02602930701562981

Frey, B. B., & Schmidt, V. L. (2007). Coming to terms with classroom assessment. *Journal of Advanced Academics, 18*(3), 402-423. https://doi.org/10.4219/jaa-2007-495

Hamp-Lyons, L. (2016). Implementing a learning-oriented approach within English language assessment in Hong Kong schools: practices, issues and complexities. In G. Yu & Y. Jin (Eds), *Assessing Chinese learners of English*. Palgrave Macmillan.

Hamp-Lyons, L., & Tavares, N. (2011). Interactive assessment – a dialogic and collaborative approach to assessing learners' oral language. In D. Tsagari & I. Csépes (Eds), *Classroom based language assessment* (pp. 29-46). Peter Lang.

Harlen, W. (2012). On the relationship between assessment for formative and summative purposes. In J. R. Gardner (Ed.), *Assessment and learning* (pp. 87-102). Sage Publications. https://doi.org/10.4135/9781446250808.n6

Hattie, J., & Timperley, H. (2007). The power of feedback. *Review of Educational Research, 77*(1), 81-112.

Inbar-Lourie, O., & Donitsa-Schmidt, S. (2009). Exploring classroom assessment practices: the case of teachers of English as a foreign language. *Assessment in Education: Principles, Policy & Practice, 16*(2), 185-204. https://doi.org/10.1080/09695940903075958

Ioannou S., & Tsagari, D. (2022a). Effects of recasts, metalinguistic feedback, and students' proficiency on the acquisition of Greek perfective past tense. *Languages, 7*(1), 40. https://doi.org/10.3390/languages7010040

Ioannou, S., & Tsagari, D. (2022b). Interactional corrective feedback in beginner level classrooms of Greek as a second language: teachers' practices. *Research Papers in Language Teaching and Learning, 12*(1), 7-25.

Lantolf, J. P., & Poehner, M. E. (2008). Dynamic assessment. In E. Shohamy & N. H. Hornberger (Eds), *Encyclopedia of language and education* (pp. 273-284). Springer.

Meletiadou, E., & Tsagari, D. (2022). Exploring teachers' perceptions of the use of peer assessment in external exam-dominated writing classes. *Languages, 7*(1), 16. https://doi.org/10.3390/languages7010016

Michaeloudes, G. (2018). Formative assessment in EFL primary schools in Cyprus. PhD thesis. University of Cyprus.

Pryor, J., & Crossouard, B. (2008). A socio-cultural theorisation of formative assessment. *Oxford Review of Education, 34*(1), 1-20.

Rea-Dickins, P. (2006). Currents and eddies in the discourse of assessment: a learning-focused interpretation. *International Journal of Applied Linguistics, 16*(2), 163-188. https://doi.org/10.1111/j.1473-4192.2006.00112.x

Rea-Dickins, P. (2008). Classroom based assessment. In E. Shohamy & N. H. Hornberger (Eds), *Encyclopedia of language and education* (pp. 1-15). Springer.

Scriven, M. (1967). The methodology of evaluation. In R. Tyler, R. Gagne & M. Scriven (Eds), *Perspectives of curriculum evaluation* (pp. 39-83). Rand McNally.

Stiggins, R. J. (2002). Assessment crisis: the absence of assessment FOR learning. *Phi Delta Kappan, 83*(10), 758-765. https://doi.org/10.1177/003172170208301010

Taras, M. (2008). Issues of power and equity in two models of self-assessment. *Teaching in Higher Education, 13*(1), 81-92. https://doi.org/10.1080/13562510701794076

Torrance, H. (2012). Formative assessment at the crossroads: conformative, deformative and transformative assessment. *Oxford Review of Education, 38*(3), 323-342.

Tsagari, D. (2014). Unplanned LOA in EFL classrooms: findings from an empirical study. *Paper presented at Roundtable on Learning-Oriented Assessment in Language Classrooms and Large-Scale Assessment Contexts, 10-12 October 2014, at Teachers College, Columbia University, New York.*

Tsagari, D. (2021). Gauging the assessment literacy levels of English teachers in Norway. *The European Journal of Applied Linguistics and TEFL, 10*(1), 161-191.

Tsagari, D., & Csépes, I. (2011). (Eds). *Classroom-based language assessment.* Peter Lang.

Tsagari, D., & Meletiadou, E. (2015). Peer assessment of adolescent learners' writing performance. *Writing & Pedagogy, 7*(2), 305-328. https://doi.org/10.1558/wap.v7i2-3.26457

Tsagari, D., & Michaeloudes, G. (2012). Formative assessment practices in private language schools in Cyprus. In D. Tsagari (Ed.), *Research on English as a foreign language in cyprus* (vol. II, pp. 246-265). University of Nicosia Press.

Tsagari, D., & Michaeloudes, G. (2013). Formative assessment patterns in CLIL primary schools in Cyprus. In D. Tsagari, S. Papadima-Sophocleous & S. Ioannou-Georgiou (Eds), *International experiences in language testing and assessment* (pp. 75-93). Peter Lang.

Tsagari, D., & Vogt, K. (2017). Assessment literacy of foreign language teachers around Europe: research, challenges and future prospects. *Papers in Language Testing and Assessment, 6*(1), 41-63.

Turner, C. E., & Purpura, J. E. (2016). Learning-oriented assessment in second and foreign language classrooms. In D. Tsagari & J. Banerjee (Eds), *Handbook of second language assessment* (pp. 255-273). DeGruyter Mouton. https://doi.org/10.1515/9781614513827-018

Turner, C. E. (2012). Classroom assessment. In G. Fulcher & F. Davidson (Eds), *The Routledge handbook of language testing* (pp. 65-78). Routledge.

Vogt, K., & Tsagari, D. (2014). Assessment literacy of foreign language teachers: findings of a European study. *Language Assessment Quarterly, 11*(4), 374-402. https://doi.org/10.1080/15434303.2014.960046

Vogt, K., Tsagari, D., & Spanoudis, G. (2020). What do teachers think they want? A comparative study of in-service language teachers' beliefs on LAL training needs. *Language Assessment Quarterly, 17*(4), 386-409. https://doi.org/10.1080/15434303.2020.1781128

Introduction

Assessment has always been part of the educational lives of the global population. This is also the case with the field of language learning. In the long history of language learning, the majority of language assessment experiences have been related to testing, and more precisely to the testing of language acquisition. Inevitably, most research publications up until early 2022 have been recording testing (e.g. Chalhoub-Deville, 2001; Fulcher, 2015; Fulcher & Harding, 2022; O'Sullivan, 2012; Spolsky, 2016). It is undeniable that testing has been accompanied by feelings of anxiety, stress, and fear of failure. It is only in recent years that Formative Assessment (FA) and assessment for learning (Rea-Dickins & Gardner, 2000; Tsagari & Vogt, 2017) were given attention. This form of assessment is usually accompanied by feelings of learning, reflection, improvement, satisfaction, and achievement, and it is worth exploring and integrating into the language learning and assessment process. Despite the increased interest in language FA over the last 20 years (e.g. Rea-Dickins & Gardner, 2000; Tsagari & Michaeloudes, 2013; Vogt & Tsagari, 2014), most research publications in the long history of language assessment focus mainly on Summative Assessment (SA), testing, and high stakes examinations and their different aspects (validity, reliability, washback, impact, etc. – see e.g. Hamp-Lyons, 1997; O'Sullivan, 2015, 2016). While acknowledging the importance of assessment, which has mainly been in the form of testing, we, the authors of this book, recognise the need to also give due attention to the history of FA in language learning. Within this frame of mind, this book moves towards this direction and attempts to provide researchers, undergraduate and postgraduate students, language practitioners, policymakers, and other stakeholders with more information and data accumulated in recent years, and more precisely between 2000 and 2020, so as to have a holistic overview of language FA research and more extensive knowledge of this domain (Rea-Dickins & Gardner, 2000; Tsagari & Michaeloudes, 2013; Vogt & Tsagari, 2014).

Introduction

An initial search revealed that there is substantial activity by researchers and language practitioners all over the world. However, there is no Systematic Review (SR) or Annotated Bibliography (AB) that is dedicated to the recording, describing, and evaluating of the historical background of implementations of FA in Second Language (L2)/Foreign Language (FL) learning. Most such publications are more generic on the contribution of FA and not related to FA in L2/FL; some literature reviews were found as parts of research papers dedicated to L2. This first finding was part of an MA in computer assisted language learning dissertation written by Skevi Vassiliou (2019) and supervised by Dr Salomi Papadima-Sophocleous (first supervisor) and Dr Christina Giannikas (second supervisor). The idea for the topic of this dissertation derived from the module on computer assisted language assessment and testing taught by Dr Salomi Papadima-Sophocleous. This collaboration led to the co-authoring of this book, which started at the end of 2019 and was completed in 2022.

As the title suggests, the book tells the story of FA in two ways, the one complementing the other: the first one is in the form of an SR and the second one is in the form of a descriptive and evaluative AB of L2 FA, from the very first published work on the subject in 2000 to 2020. While the SR gives the story of language FA in chronological order and gives an overview of different aspects, the AB gives more details for each research work.

The main purposes of this book are: (1) to provide researchers, practitioners, and other stakeholders interested in language FA a substantial background in the area, (2) to describe how this topic has been approached by researchers worldwide over the 20 years under review, (3) to contribute to the development of critical thinking about the topic, (4) to help in establishing the relevance and quality of the annotated material on the topic, and (5) to facilitate language formative researchers as well as practitioners to form an overview of the research in the area during the specific period under study.

The first part synthesises different studies related to language FA, from 2000 to 2020. It shares insights into the types of publications researched, the research purposes, the type of research designs, the research methods and data collection tools used in the studies, the research outcomes, the languages, types of participants and educational levels represented in the publications, the types of FA applications, the language learning focus formatively assessed, the learning theories and teaching methods used to FA in LL, and the geographic distribution of these studies.

The second part consists of a series of bibliographical citations and entries. This descriptive and evaluative AB of language FA is organised in chronological order from 2000 to 2020; it shows step-by-step progress through the years; it is based on a list of inclusion/exclusion criteria and a list of evaluative criteria; it includes 104 annotations; it presents research that has been conducted each year. Each annotation describes and evaluates the content of each publication.

This book complements the literature so far written on language assessment in general. It focuses on FA, which comparatively to research conducted for SA in LL, requires further investigation. It comes to fill the gap that exists by giving an overview of the research in language FA activities in the last 20 years since FA started making an appearance within the language learning context.

The first step towards that was to have an overview of what constitutes FA in general, and in LL in particular, and establish the characteristics of an SR and an AB.

References

Chalhoub-Deville, M. (2001). Language testing and technology: past and future. *Language Learning & Technology, 5*(2), 95-98. https://doi.org/10125/25130

Fulcher, G. (2015). *Re-examining language testing: a philosophical and social inquiry.* Routledge. https://doi.org/10.4324/9781315695518

Fulcher, G., & Harding, L. (2022). *The Routledge handbook of language testing* (2nd ed.). Routledge. https://doi.org/10.4324/9781003220756

Hamp-Lyons, L. (1997). Washback, impact and validity: ethical concerns. *Language Testing, 14*(3), 295-303. https://doi.org/10.1177/026553229701400306

Introduction

O'Sullivan, B. (2012). A brief history of language testing. In C. Coombe, P. Davidson, B. O'Sullivan, & C. Stoynoff (Eds), *The Cambridge guide to language assessment* (pp. 9-19). Cambridge University Press.

O'Sullivan, B. (2015). Validity, validation and development: building and operationalizing a comprehensive model. *Japanese Language Testing Association Journal, 18,* 25-33. https://doi.org/10.20622/jltajournal.18.0_25

O'Sullivan, B. (2016). Validity: what is it and who is It for? In Yiu-nam Leung (Ed.), *Epoch making in English teaching and learning: evolution, innovation, and revolution* (pp.157-175). Crane Publishing Company.

Rea-Dickins, P., & Gardner, S. (2000). Snares and silver bullets: disentangling the construct of formative assessment. *Language Testing, 17*(2), 215-243. https://doi.org/10.1177/026553220001700206

Spolsky, B. (2016). History of language testing. In E. Shohamy, I. Or & S. May (Eds), *Language testing and assessment. Encyclopedia of language and education* (3rd ed.). Springer. https://doi.org/10.1007/978-3-319-02326-7_32-1

Tsagari, D., & Michaeloudes, G. (2013). Formative assessment patterns in CLIL primary schools in Cyprus. In S. Ioannou-Georgiou, S. Papadima-Sophocleous & D. Tsagari (Eds), *International experiences in language testing and assessment* (pp. 75-93). Peter Lang Edition.

Tsagari, D., & Vogt, K. (2017). Assessment literacy of foreign language teachers around Europe: research, challenges and future prospects. *Papers in Language Testing and Assessment, 6*(1), 41-63. https://www.researchgate.net/publication/316981583_Assessment_Literacy_of_Foreign_Language_Teachers_around_Europe_Research_Challenges_and_Future_Prospects

Vassiliou, S. (2019). *Formative assessment in second language learning: a systematic review and an annotated bibliography.* Master's thesis. Cyprus University of Technology. https://ktisis.cut.ac.cy/handle/10488/22825

Vogt, K., & Tsagari, D. (2014). Assessment literacy of foreign language teachers: findings of a European study. *Language Assessment Quarterly, 11*(4), 374-402. https://doi.org/10.1080/15434303.2014.960046

*I cannot teach anybody anything.
I can only make them think.*

Socrates

PART 1

Formative assessment in review

This part presents the main characteristics of Formative Assessment (FA) with an emphasis on Language Learning (LL). It also exhibits the features of a Systematic Review (SR) and an Annotated Bibliography (AB) selected for the needs of this book. The aim is to set the background for the SR and AB on FA in LL, which is the focus of this book.

1.1. FA

Most of the history of assessment in education traces back to the Imperial Chinese system of examinations (Spolsky, 2008), which deals with testing. As Spolsky (2008) has argued, "language testing grew up against this background" (p. 5). Consequently, the developments and discussions about the history of language assessment deal mostly with the history of testing. A good example is O'Sullivan's (2012) chapter *A Brief History of Language Testing* (pp. 9-19).

Testing and assessment are often treated as synonyms. This is evident in cases, where the word *assessment*, and/or *testing* are used in publications' titles but in reality, the publication concentrates on testing. The following examples are indicative: Davies's (2013) *Fifty years of language assessment;* Spolsky's (2016) *Language assessment in historical and future perspective*; and Farhady's (2018) *History of language testing and assessment.*

In its history, language assessment has followed the developments in assessment in education and in theory. As described by Farhady (2018), various perspectives and issues resulted in drastic changes and in shifting the attention to finding alternatives to assessing language ability in the context of and during the process of learning. One could observe this over the years as assessment moved from the prescientific to the scientific, structuralist, integrative sociolinguistic to the communicative era of language teaching and learning, and faced pedagogical implications. It moved from what the student knows to what the student can do. These alternative types of learning involved student cooperation, the assumption of more responsibility in their learning, and encouraged the application of knowledge to solving real-life problems. Alternative assessment goes beyond traditional forms of assessment such as tests and high-stakes examinations. Similarly, FA evaluates during the process in the form of, for example, classroom polls, exit tickets, and early feedback, and not in the form of midterm exams, end-of-unit or chapter tests, final projects or papers, district benchmark and scores, after the learning process as SA does; FA monitors the learning process rather than assigning grades, it aims to improve student's learning rather than evaluating student's achievements, it focuses on little content areas rather than complete chapters or content areas, and it considers evaluations as a process and not as a product as summative assessment does (Renard, 2017).

For the purposes of this book, we first examine the various definitions of FA and its characteristics given in the course of its history; the aim of this was to establish a definition that incorporates the most common characteristics discussed by researchers, which could then be the base for the SR and AB which constitute parts of this book.

Scriven (1967) was the first to suggest two roles evaluation may play. He suggested that evaluation

> "may have a role in the on-going improvement of the curriculum [... and] may serve to enable administrators to decide whether the entire finished curriculum refined by the use of the evaluation process in its first role, represents a sufficiently significant advance on the available alternatives to justify the expense of adoption by a school system" (Scriven, 1967, pp. 41-42).

To define these two roles in relation to curriculum evaluation and distinguish their differences, he proposed "the terms 'Formative' and 'Summative' evaluation" (Scriven, 1967, p. 43).

Not long after Scriven's (1967) definitions, Bloom (1969) stated that the same terms can be used not only to evaluate curriculum but also to evaluate students' learning. While acknowledging the value of summative evaluation of student learning, Bloom (1969) has also emphasised the value of formative evaluation. He saw 'formative evaluation' as a way "to provide feedback and correctness at each stage in the teaching-learning process" (Bloom, 1969, p. 48). Both Scriven (1967) and Bloom (1969) supported that the information given during formative evaluation helps in making changes in the teaching and learning activities during the learning process.

Since then, a lot of other researchers have attempted to define SA and FA and their differences. Saito and Inoi (2017) support that some classroom assessments, such as midterms, finals, and large-scale achievement tests, are 'inherently' summative because they are administered with summative intention, whereas most other types of classroom assessments are inherently formative. According to Bennett (2011) and Liu (2015), SA is a one-time opportunity where a student can demonstrate their knowledge. Brookhart (2010) maintains that the division between FA and SA is still blurred, as assessment can be used for both summative and formative purposes.

Black and Wiliam have been contributing to the evolution of FA since the 1990's. Their wide-ranging literature review claimed that "conclusively [...] FA does improve learning" (Black & Wiliam, 1998, p. 61). They identified the main features of FA as sharing criteria with learners, developing classroom talk and questioning, giving appropriate feedback, and peer and self-assessment. In their review, FA "is to be interpreted as encompassing all those activities undertaken by teachers, and/or by their students, which provide information to be used as feedback to modify the teaching and learning activities in which they are engaged" (Black & Wiliam, 1998, pp. 7-8). Black and Wiliam (1998) and Boston (2002) referred to FA as ongoing: during the assessment process, teachers gather evidence of the student's learning, which they use to adapt their teaching so that it meets students' needs and diagnoses their progress toward a long-term objective.

FA has been described as an 'assessment for learning', while SA has been defined as an 'assessment of learning' (Rea-Dickins & Gardner, 2000). This means that students need to be given continuous information about their own learning, how they are progressing, the nature, scope, and level of their learning, and in which areas improvement is needed. Both types of assessment are equally valuable and significant in the learning process and complement each other. Gattullo (2000, p. 279) characterised FA as an ongoing multi-phase process that is carried out on a daily basis through teacher-pupil interaction with the provision of feedback.

'Assessment for learning' has also been described as "the process of seeking and interpreting evidence for use by learners and their teachers to decide where the learners are in their learning, where they need to go and how best to get there" (Broadfoot et al., 2002, p. 3). In Wiliam (2011), 'assessment for learning' is defined as "any assessment for which the first priority in its design and practice is to serve the purpose of promoting students' learning. It thus differs from assessment designed primarily to serve the purposes of accountability, or of ranking, or of certifying competence" (p. 10). Stiggins (2005) recognised FA as a diagnostic test, however, Popham (2006) argued that FA is not a test, it is a process. Cizek (2010) has claimed that not all these characteristics should be met in order for assessment to be formative. According to Black and Wiliam (2018), the teacher elicits "evidence of students' understanding and based on that evidence takes decision for next steps for effective instruction" (p. 8). Teachers need to be aware of what students understand from the learning experience. Tan (2013) also aimed "to identify the minimal requirements for FA to succeed in terms of assessment standards, assessment design, and assessment feedback" (p. 1). Bahati, Tedre, Fors, and Evode (2016) support that assessment can only be considered *formative* if it can generate feedback that students can use to improve their learning and achievements. Additionally, it also needs to be used by teachers to re-evaluate and reflect on teaching strategies in response to their learners' needs, which means FA occurs during the course of learning. It aims to determine the next steps by giving feedback to students and establishing students' needs and progress in order to modify aspects such as planning, curriculum design, content, learning experiences, and resources for the benefit of students' learning. It has been practised much less and only in the last decades during the history of assessment (Heineke & McTighe, 2018).

FA is an informal type of assessment, as opposed to formal assessment. Formal assessment typically means a test or examination that involves standardised administration, for example, end-of-chapter tests, end-of-semester tests, or high-stakes examinations. Informal assessment is a process of obtaining information that can be used to make judgements about students' progress and make improvements in the learning processes. Informal assessments include, e.g. projects, presentations, experiments, demonstrations, or performances (Ketabi & Ketabi, 2014). They can include portfolios, asking questions during class, or informal observations of interaction, quizzes, rubrics, discussions, and self and peer assessment techniques (Ketabi & Ketabi, 2014) for FA purposes in order to improve the learning processes and learning.

In reality, FA is considered an alternative type of assessment, which refers to assessments, alternative to traditional ones, that offer a variety of measurement ways designed to understand what a student can do rather than what they know. Alternative assessment measures proficiency in relation to knowledge application rather than recitation or memorisation and includes designated projects, portfolios, observations, performance tasks, exhibitions, demonstrations, journals, reflective pieces, case-based scenarios, reports, teacher-created tests, rubrics, and self- and peer-evaluation. Bahrani (2011) also mentions interviews and the implementation of a number of Web 2.0 tools. They encourage critical thinking, collaboration, and information synthesis. They derive, reflect, and focus more on what learners can do in authentic-like real-life like, contextualised tasks (Papadima-Sophocleous, 2017). Moreover, the elements of alternative assessment can provide the learner with the opportunity to show what they can do with the language with innovative teaching approaches and techniques (Rea-Dickins, 2004), learning experiences, resources, modified curriculum design,

Part 1

and content; this process can be characterised as a response to the traditional test-based assessment.

FA is also considered a classroom assessment approach. According to this type of assessment, teachers attempt to find out what and how well the learners understand during the lesson and to improve the quality of students' learning by making new decisions, which would facilitate improvement in the learning process (Angelo & Cross, 2012). According to Heineke and McTighe (2018), the following have been recorded as used for FA purposes: formal data collection such as quizzes, academic prompts, and second informal like classroom observations, dialogues, self-, and peer-assessment checks for understanding. Teachers integrate multiple opportunities to collect evidence in order to monitor learners' progress throughout the learning process. Black and Wiliam (2009) mention in their article *Developing the theory of formative assessment*, FA can also give rise to effective changes with the integration of interactive feedback.

Since Black and Wiliam's (2009) review on classroom assessment and learning was published, the authors continuously contributed in the area of assessment. In one of their latest publications (Black & Wiliam, 2018), they propose a model design of educational activities and argue that assessment is influenced by a combination of the theories of pedagogy, instruction, learning, and the subject discipline, along with the wider context of education. This indicates that FA practices are considered as one of the most motivational modes to increase students' engagement and performance (Ketabi & Ketabi, 2014). In their critical review of research on FA, Dunn and Mulvenon (2009) have tried to capture the scientific evidence of the impact of FA in education. They have argued that, although FA is important, limited empirical evidence exists to support the 'best practises' for formative evaluation.

1.2. FA in LL

The first publication that referred to FA in LL was by Rea-Dickins and Gardner in 2000. Before the year 2000, not much had been recorded regarding FA in

LL, neglect noted by Rea-Dickins and Gardner (2000). In the year 2000, Rea-Dickins and Gardner put emphasis on the characteristics of FA. They argued that if teachers' decisions are made responsibly during the language lesson, this will increase students' performance (Rea-Dickins & Gardner, 2000). Cheng, Rogers, and Hu (2004) also argued that the study of the assessment practices in the field of English LL and teaching were limited. The claims of neglect continued when Fakeye (2016) stated that FA is an overlooked type of assessment since language teachers pay more attention to SA that includes tests and scores. After the year 2000, studies began to focus on FA and English as a Second Language/English as a Foreign Language (ESL/EFL) and paid more attention to aspects such as the process and design of learning, the curriculum design, the learning experiences, content, and planning teachers needed to employ for this type of assessment. Bachman and Palmer were among the first who mentioned that giving feedback to language students may support their performance in formal tests. They also emphasised the relationship between FA and formal tests in language education (Bachman & Palmer, 2010).

Gradually, FA started being globally recognised as an essential element in the language area; however, it continued to face implementation issues and the need for more research continued to be evident. Heitink et al. (2016), for instance, have argued that there is limited scientific evidence on the positive impact of FA. Additionally, the different conceptualisations of FA and their understanding made FA applications more difficult and the research of FA applications in LL more challenging. At the same time, FA faced some practical issues; for example, emphasis was put by teachers who were used to practicing SA, marking and scores, especially in crowded classes instead of providing feedback, and did not agree on how FA is given (Ketabi & Ketabi, 2014).

As pedagogy progressed with time, the integration of technology in education added opportunities for a supportive environment to implement FA practices for LL, provided it is aligned with the learning theory, language teaching/learning, and FA principles (Vassiliou & Papadima-Sophocleous, 2019). Technology-enhanced teaching and learning allow the teacher and the learner to use a number of tools for FA purposes that would enable to increase the

L2 learning outcomes (Perera-Diltz & Moe, 2014). Technology-enhanced learning can accommodate better environments for effective, instant, and meaningful feedback (Heinrich, Milne, & Moore, 2009), depending on its nature and quality. Furthermore, the proliferation of technology tools in L2 has the potential to support the role of FA and enable learners and educators to use technologies not only for score tests and exams but also for meaningful FA. E-assessment tools, like online quizzes, can also be used following the FA principles and provide comprehensive and on-time feedback to students, and most interestingly they can monitor their understanding (Baleni, 2015). According to the literature, examples of e-tools that can be used for FA purposes and can provide e-feedback are: (1) Turnitin and Grademark, (2) Electronic Feedback Software, (3) Questionmark Perception, (4) WebCTConnect, (5) MarkTool, (6) Markin (http://www.cict.co.uk/software/markin/index.htm), (7) Moodle Quiz, and (8) Markers Assistant (Heinrich et al., 2009). Another example of an online tool that offers the opportunity for instant and effective feedback and can be used for FA purposes, is Google Docs where teachers and students can discuss and exchange ideas synchronously on a shared document (Reimann, Halb, Bull, & Johnson, 2011).

Additionally, other e-applications offer opportunities to students for self and peer feedback as part of FA like the Online Peer Feedback (OPF) application, (Rosalia & Llosa, 2009). Furthermore, it has been argued that there are some technology-enhanced tools that can be used to support FA integrations. Examples of such tools include e-journals, e-reflections, e-portfolios, e-rubrics, e-can-do lists, and e-artefacts, with the use of Google documents and Google Sites (Papadima-Sophocleous, 2017). Google Forms can also be used as an excellent type of e-Exit ticket cards and/or as a type of self-reflections. Responses from such tools assist teachers in their planning of subsequent lessons according to students' understanding (Exit Ticket, n.d.).

According to the literature, the use of iPods and iPads can be used for FA in LL (Levy & Gertler, 2015; Medina & Hurtado, 2017). Students can make videos or audio recordings and improve their speaking and listening skills. Many studies highlight the importance of gamified quizzes and online assessment tools like

Socrative, Kahoot, Eclipse, Quizlet, Edmodo, Padlet, Storify, Google Doc, Google Forms, and Remind 101 as FA tools in LL, which can be used during the learning process, and give instant feedback to students; in order to modify and improve their curriculum design, content, their student's learning experiences and their learning (Heinrich et al., 2009; Reimann et al., 2011).

As established so far, FA is both conceptually and practically still shaping. However, in order to proceed in conducting an SR and an AB which focus on FA, some foundation needed to be set. According to Bennett (2011, p. 6), in order to provide the field with a meaningful definition of FA, we need (1) a theory of action and (2) a concrete instantiation. The theory of action can identify the characteristics and components of the entity we are claiming FA is, along with a rationale for each characteristic and component; and proposes how these characteristics and components can work together in order to create a desired set of outcomes.

Our theory of action stems from the literature review we conducted regarding different stands on FA, and revolves around the idea of involving both students and teachers during the students' learning: engaging in effective discussions, interaction, criteria development, giving feedback, engaging in teacher, self and peer assessment, and gathering evidence of learner's learning, which they would use to adapt both the teaching and the learning in order to diagnose students' needs and progress in a continuum, toward a long-term objective.

For the purpose of this book, we have adopted the following FA features, drawn from earlier research, in the hope that each reviewed and annotated publication would fully or partially reflect them.

FA characteristics taken into consideration in this volume are as follows.

- It is classroom (Can Daşkın & Hatipoğlu, 2019) and school based in contrast to high-stakes examinations which are externally based.

- It involves students, the teacher, and peers (Carless, 2002).

- It supports learning and assessment for forming learning in many ways; the theoretical background of FA is aligned with current learning theories, such as constructivism. Constructivist learning practices, for example, are in line with the nature of formative evaluation as described by Stiggins (2005), stating that formative evaluations enable learning to be guided according to the student's ability level. It provides students with opportunities for active involvement in their own learning in an environment where both students and teachers are engaged (Heitink et al., 2016).

- It is part of the learning and teaching process, it gathers information from them (Gan & Leung, 2020; Shepard, 2006) to further improve "the instructional decisions that are made by teachers, learners" (Wiliam, 2011, p. 13) or their peers, unlike SA which is usually administered to categorise students' performances or for accreditation (Cizek, 2010, p. 1).

- It helps students "understand learning objectives and become aware of strategies and steps to be undertaken in order to move their learning forward" (Gan & Leung, 2020, p. 2).

- It provides opportunities for giving feedback by an agent (e.g. teacher, peer, self), engaging in teacher, self and peer assessment, and gathering evidence of learner's learning, which they would use to adapt both the teaching and the learning in order to diagnose students' needs and progress in a continuum, toward a long-term objective (Bachman & Palmer, 2010).

- It establishes what students know while they are still in the process of learning it (Broadfoot et al., 2002).

- It materialises in classroom-based practices that range from e.g. observations, class discussions, peer- and self-assessment, feedback, moment-by-moment teacher decisions and responses, and construction of artefacts, etc. These can be in paper or technology and web-based FA form, with the latter offering interactivity, real-time practice, multimedia features, timely feedback, variety of formative exercises, own pace learning, provision of multiple attempts (Buchanan, 2000; Jia, Chen, Ding, & Ruan, 2012), and gaming features and strategies (Wang, 2008).

- It includes a collection of evidence of performances over time to provide evidence of growth and learning; it is closely related to teachers' day-to-day work of teaching and learning and assessment *for* learning (Scarino, 2013, p. 312).

- It supports and facilitates the process of learning before SA comes to verify at the end of a learning process what learning has been achieved and whether the learning outcomes have been met.

As one can observe, the FA and SA boundaries are not clear. Some assessment applications can be used in both. What needs to be clear is that it is the purpose of the assessment that helps in defining and determining whether it is formative or summative. The above features aim to assist in deciding when the intention is to assess students formally.

The examination of the research conducted so far on FA has established that the definition of FA is not yet completed, it is in its making. However, in order to record both in the SR and the AB the research activities in the area of FA in LL during the designated period, we had to come up with a minimum framework of the main characteristics of FA as discussed so far in the literature. With the recording of the sources between 2000 and 2020, however, we established that this is an area that offers itself for further future research.

So far, we have presented the characteristics of FA in general and described its presence and contribution in LL in particular. Preliminary research helped in establishing that there is no comprehensive SR, nor any AB in FA in LL.

The results revealed the existence of some literature reviews as a part of research papers, or more generic research focused on FA implications and not on FA and LL (Allal & Lopez, 2005; Black & Wiliam, 1998; Dunn & Mulvenon, 2009; Gikandi, Morrow, & Davis, 2011). As a result, the aim of this research was to examine the area of FA in LL through first an SR and then an AB in FA in LL in order to establish a more solid background in the area. In order to conduct an SR and an AB, an investigation of their characteristics was conducted in order to clearly set the parameters of the study.

1.3. SR

An SR is based on a research review design and can be of a qualitative, quantitative and/or mixed research approach. The main purpose of SR is to synthesise different studies which are related to a specific research area (Hanley & Cutts, 2013). SR is different from a narrative traditional type of research as it critically summarises and synthesises all data related to a topic, and focuses on systematic research of the literature (Štrukelj, 2018). As with other research designs, SR follows a specific protocol, meaning it has a set of characteristics that one follows. Some of these characteristics are: (1) a clearly stated set of objectives; (2) a presentation of one or more research questions; (3) an explicit, reproducible methodology; (4) a set of clearly defined criteria for inclusion/exclusion of the relevant studies; (5) a systematic search for identification of studies that would meet the eligibility criteria; (6) a systematic presentation and synthesis of the findings, making comparisons, associations, or identifications of new research areas; and (7) assessment of the validity of the findings (Hanley & Cutts, 2013). According to Norris and Ortega (2007), the strengths of systematically reviewing applied linguistics are promising, in comparison to narrative literature reviews. It can reveal gaps, weaknesses, and needs in a research area. For that reason, Norris and Ortega (2007) encourage applied linguists to adopt this research design and "to think and act systematically" (p. 813).

The above research review design characteristics and guidelines were followed in Part 2 of this book to conduct the SR on FA in LL.

1.4. AB

An AB provides an overview of available research sources (Engle, 2017), of the main issues, arguments, and research within a particular area. This list of works is formatted according to a specific documentation style (e.g. MLA, APA, etc.) (Saint Mary's University, 2019). The content of the AB can be listed alphabetically by the author or arranged chronologically by publication date. In the introduction, the topic or subject area covered by the bibliography is described, and the method used to identify possible sources, the rationale for selecting the sources, and, if appropriate, an explanation describing the reasons for exclusions of some types of resources are explained (Harner, 2015). This introduction is then followed by the citation, according to the specific chosen documentation style, followed by an annotation, a summative paragraph that evaluatively describes the content of the source.

An AB focuses on the importance of each source in relation to the topic (Buttram, MacMillan, & Koch, 2012). It pays particular attention to the content and contribution of each individual source to the given area of research. Each entry can be defined as a brief explanatory or evaluative note of each reference or citation (Buttram et al., 2012). An annotation can be helpful to researchers in informing them about the source and evaluating whether the source is relevant to a given topic or line of inquiry (Engle, 2017).

The above characteristics and guidelines were followed in Part 3 of this book to conduct the AB on FA in LL.

1.5. Why combine SR and AB?

The reason for combining the two different research designs conducted during the specific time period under study was to give as much information as possible about the publications on FA in LL. The research is based on specific research questions, and a systematic evaluation of FA in LL studies of 2000-2020, with the use of inclusion and exclusion criteria. The aims were:

- to synthesise, analyse, and interpret all the data by making comparisons, associations, or identifying new research areas (Hanley & Cutts, 2013); and

- to then focus on the importance of each source in relation to the topic (Buttram et al., 2012), pay particular attention to the content and contribution of each individual source, by briefly describing and evaluating explanatorily each reference or citation (Buttram et al., 2012).

The first step towards that was to have an overview of this activity through an SR of the research carried out during this period.

References

Allal, L., & Lopez, L. M. (2005). Formative assessment of learning: a review of publications in French. In J. Looney (Ed.), *Formative assessment: improving learning in secondary classrooms* (pp. 241-264). Organisation for Economic Cooperation and Development. http://www.oecd.org/edu/ceri/34488354.pdf

Angelo, T. A., & Cross, K. P. (2012). *Classroom assessment techniques*. Jossey Bass Wiley.

Bachman, L. F., & Palmer, A. S. (2010). *Language assessment in practice: developing language assessments and justifying their use in the real world*. Oxford University Press.

Bahati, B., Tedre, M., Fors, U., & Evode, M. (2016). Exploring feedback practises in formative assessment in Rwandan higher education: a multifaceted approach is needed. *International Journal of Teaching and Education, 4*(2), 1-22. https://doi.org/10.20472/TE.2016.4.2.001

Bahrani, T. (2011). Technology as an assessment tool in language learning. *International Journal of English Linguistics, 1*(2), 295-298. https://doi.org/10.5539/ijel.v1n2p295

Baleni, Z. G. (2015). Online formative assessment in higher education: its pros and cons. *The Electronic Journal of e-Learning, 13*(4), 228-236. https://academic-publishing.org/index.php/ejel/article/view/1730

Bennett, R. E. (2011). Formative assessment: a critical review. *Assessment in Education: Principles, Policy & Practice, 18*(1), 5-25. https://doi.org/10.1080/0969594X.2010.513678

Black, P., & Wiliam, D. (1998). Assessment and classroom learning. *Assessment in Education, Principles, Policy & Practice, 5*(1), 7-74. https://doi.org/10.1080/0969595980050102

Black, P., & Wiliam, D. (2009). Developing the theory of formative assessment. *Educational Assessment, Evaluation and Accountability, 21*(1), 5-31. https://doi.org/10.1007/s11092-008-9068-5

Black, P., & Wiliam, D. (2018). Classroom assessment and pedagogy. *Assessment in education: principles, policy & practice, 25*(6), 551-575. DOI: https://doi.org/10.1080/0969594X.2018.1441807

Bloom, B. S. (1969). Some theoretical issues relating to educational evaluation. In R. W. Tyler (Ed.), *Educational evaluation: new toles, new means: the 63rd yearbook of the National Society for the Study of Education, part 2* (pp. 26-50). University of Chicago Press.

Boston, C. (2002). The concept of formative assessment. *Practical Assessment, Research & Evaluation, 8*(9), 1-4. https://doi.org/10.7275/kmcq-dj31

Broadfoot, P., Daugherty, R., Gardner, J., Harlen, W., James, M., & Stobart G. (2002). *Assessment for learning: 10 principles. Assessment Reform Group*. Nuffield Foundation and University of Cambridge. http://assessmentreformgroup.files.wordpress.com/2012/01/10principles_english.pdf

Brookhart, S. M. (2010). Mixing it up: combining sources of classroom achievement information for formative and summative purposes. In H. L. Andrade & G. J. Cizek (Eds), *Handbook of formative assessment* (pp. 279-296). Routledge.

Buchanan, T. (2000). The efficacy of a World-Wide Web mediated formative assessment. *Journal of Computer Assisted Learning, 16*(3), 193-200. https://doi.org/10.1046/j.1365-2729.2000.00132.x

Buttram, C., MacMillan, D., & Koch, R.T. (2012). *Comparing the annotated bibliography to the literature review*. UNA Center for Writing excellence. https://www.una.edu/writingcenter/docs/Writing-Resources/Comparing%20the%20Annotated%20Bibliography%20to%20the%20Literature%20Review.pdf

Can Daşkın, N., & Hatipoğlu, Ç. (2019). Reference to a past learning event as a practice of informal formative assessment in L2 classroom interaction. *Language Testing, 36*(4), 527-551. https://doi.org/10.1177/0265532219857066

Carless, D. R. (2002). The mini-viva as a tool to enhance assessment for learning. *Assessment & Evaluation in Higher Education, 27*(4), 353-363. https://doi.org/10.1080/0260293022000001364

Cheng, L., Rogers, T., & Hu, H. (2004). ESL/EFL instructors' classroom assessment practices: purposes, methods, and procedures. *Language Testing, 21*(3), 360-389. https://doi.org/10.1191/0265532204lt288oa

Cizek, G. (2010). An introduction to formative assessment. In H. Andrade & G. Cizek (Eds), *Handbook of formative assessment* (1st ed., pp. 3-17). Routledge. https://www.routledge.com/Handbook-of-Formative-Assessment/Andrade-Cizek/p/book/9780415993203

Davies, A. (2013). Fifty years of language assessment. In A. J. Kunan (Ed.), *The companion to language assessment* (pp. 1-21). Wiley-Blackwell. https://doi.org/10.1002/9781118411360.wbcla127

Dunn, K. E., & Mulvenon, S. W. (2009). A critical review of research on formative assessment: the limited scientific evidence of the impact of formative assessment in education. *Practical Assessment, Research & Evaluation, 14*(7), 1-11. https://doi.org/10.7275/jg4h-rb87

Engle, M. (2017). *How to prepare an annotated bibliography: the annotated bibliography*. Cornell University Library. https://guides.library.cornell.edu/annotatedbibliography

Exit Ticket. (n.d.). The teacher tool kit. http://www.theteachertoolkit.com/index.php/tool/exit-ticket

Fakeye, D. O. (2016). Secondary school teachers' and students' attitudes towards formative assessment and corrective feedback in English language in Ibadan Metropolis. *Journal of Educational and Social Research, 6*(2), 141-148. https://doi.org/10.5901/jesr.2016.v6n2p141

Farhady, H. (2018). History of language testing and assessment. In J. I. Liontas (Ed.), *The TESOL encyclopedia of English language teaching* (1st ed., pp. 1-7). John Wiley & Sons. https://doi.org/10.1002/9781118784235.eelt0343

Gan, Z., & Leung, C. (2020). Illustrating formative assessment in task-based language teaching. *ELT Journal, 74*(1), 10-19. https://doi.org/10.1093/ELT/CCZ048

Gattullo, F. (2000). Formative assessment in ELT primary (elementary) classrooms: an Italian case study. *Language Testing, 17*(2), 278-288. https://doi.org/10.1177/026553220001700210

Gikandi, J. W., Morrow, D., & Davis, N. E. (2011). Online formative assessment in higher education: a review of the literature. *Computers & Education, 57*(4), 2333-2351. https://doi.org/10.1016/j.compedu.2011.06.004

Hanley, T., & Cutts, L. A. (2013). What is a systematic review? *Counselling Psychology Review, 28*(4), 3-6. https://www.research.manchester.ac.uk/portal/files/32908640/FULL_TEXT.PDF

Harner, J. L. (2015). *On compiling an annotated bibliography* (2nd ed.). Modern Language Association of America.

Heineke, A. J., & McTighe, J. (2018). *Using understanding by design in the culturally and linguistically diverse classroom*. ASCD.

Heinrich, E., Milne, J. D., & Moore, M. (2009). An Investigation into e-tool use for formative assignment assessment-status and recommendations. *Educational Technology & Society*, *12*(4), 176-192. https://www.researchgate.net/publication/220017580_An_Investigation_into_E-Tool_Use_for_Formative_Assignment_Assessment_-_Status_and_Recommendations

Heitink, M. C., Van der Kleij, F. M., Veldkamp, B. P., Schildkamp, K., & Kippers, W. B. (2016). A systematic review of prerequisites for implementing assessment for learning in classroom practice. *Educational Research Review*, *17*, 50-62. https://doi.org/10.1016/j.edurev.2015.12.002

Jia, J., Chen, Y., Ding, Z., & Ruan, M. (2012). Effects of a vocabulary acquisition and assessment system on students' performance in a blended learning class for English subject. *Computers & Education*, *58*(1), 63-76.

Ketabi, S., & Ketabi, S. (2014). Classroom and formative assessment in second/foreign language teaching and learning. *Theory & Practice in Language Studies*, *4*(2), 435-440. https://doi.org/10.4304/tpls.4.2.435-440

Levy, T., & Gertler, H. (2015). Harnessing technology to assess oral communication in Business English. *Teaching English with Technology*, *15*(4), 52-59. https://files.eric.ed.gov/fulltext/EJ1138436.pdf

Liu, X. (2015). The application of formative assessment in College English Teaching. *Proceedings of the 1st International Conference on Arts, Design and Contemporary Education* (pp. 875-879). ICADCE, 2015. https://doi.org/10.2991/icadce-15.2015.211

Medina, E. G., & Hurtado, C. (2017). Kahoot! A digital tool for learning vocabulary in a language classroom. *Revista Publicando*, *4*(12), 441-449.

Norris, J. M., & Ortega, L. (2007). The future of research synthesis in applied linguistics: beyond art or science. *TESOL Quarterly*, *41*(4), 805-815. http://www.jstor.org/stable/40264408

O'Sullivan, B. (2012). A brief history of language testing. In C. Coombe, P. Davidson, B. O'Sullivan, & C. Stoynoff (Eds), *The Cambridge guide to language assessment* (pp. 9-19). Cambridge University Press.

Papadima-Sophocleous, S. (2017). L2 assessment and testing teacher education: an exploration of alternative assessment approaches using new technologies. In K. Borthwick, L. Bradley & S. Thouësny (Eds), *CALL in a climate of change: adapting to turbulent global conditions – short papers from EUROCALL 2017* (pp. 248-253). Research-publishing.net. https://doi.org/10.14705/rpnet.2017.eurocall2017.721

Perera-Diltz, D. M., & Moe, J. L. (2014). Formative and summative assessment in online education. *Journal of Research in Innovative Teaching, 7*(1), 130-142. https://digitalcommons.odu.edu/chs_pubs/37/

Popham, W. J. (2006). Phony formative assessments: buyer beware! *Educational Leadership, 64*(3), 86-87.

Rea-Dickins, P. (2004). Understanding teachers as agents of assessment. *Language Testing, 21*(3), 249-258. https://doi.org/10.1191/0265532204lt283ed

Rea-Dickins, P., & Gardner, S. (2000). Snares and silver bullets: disentangling the construct of formative assessment. *Language Testing, 17*(2), 215-243. https://doi.org/10.1177/026553220001700206

Reimann, P., Halb, W., Bull, S., & Johnson, M. (2011). *Design of a computer-assisted assessment system for classroom formative assessment* [Conference paper]. *2011 14th International Conference on Interactive Collaborative Learning* (pp. 465-472). IEEE. https://doi.org/10.1109/ICL.2011.6059627

Renard, L. (2017). The differences between formative and summative assessment – BookWidgets interactive learning. https://www.bookwidgets.com/blog/2017/04/the-differences-between-formative-and-summative-assessment-infographic

Rosalia, C., & Llosa, L. (2009). Assessing the quality of online peer feedback in L2 writing. In R. de Cássia Veiga Marriott & P. Lupion Torres (Eds), *Handbook of research on e-learning methodologies for language acquisition* (pp. 322-338). IGI Global. https://doi.org/10.4018/978-1-59904-994-6.ch020

Saint Mary's University. (2019). *Annotated bibliographies*. https://www.smu.ca/academics/writing-an-annotated-bibliography.html

Saito, H., & Inoi, S. I. (2017). Junior and senior high school EFL teachers' use of formative assessment: a mixed-methods study. *Language Assessment Quarterly, 14*(3), 213-233. https://doi.org/10.1080/15434303.2017.1351975

Scarino, A. (2013). Language assessment literacy as self-awareness: understanding the role of interpretation in assessment and in teacher learning. *Language Testing, 30*(3), 309-327. https://doi.org/10.1177/0265532213480128

Scriven, M. (1967). The methodology of evaluation. In R. Tyler, R. Gagné & M. Scriven (Eds), *Perspectives of curriculum evaluation (AERA Monograph Series on Curriculum Evaluation* no. 1 (pp. 39-83). Rand McNally.

Shepard, L. A. (2006). Classroom assessment. In R. L. Brennan (Ed.), *Educational measurement* (4th ed., pp. 623-646). Praeger.

Spolsky, B. (2008). Language assessment in historical and future perspective. In E. Shohamy & N. H. Hornberger (Eds), *Encyclopedia of language and education* (pp. 445-454). Springer. https://doi.org/10.1007/978-0-387-30424-3_192

Spolsky, B. (2016). History of language testing. In E. Shohamy, I. Or & S. May (Eds), *Language testing and assessment. Encyclopedia of language and education* (3rd ed.). Springer. https://doi.org/10.1007/978-3-319-02326-7_32-1

Stiggins, R. (2005). From formative assessment to assessment for learning: a path to success in standards-based schools. *Phi Delta Kappan, 87*(4), 324-328. https://doi.org/10.1177/003172170508700414

Štrukelj, E. (2018, January 3). Writing a systematic literature review. *JEPS Bulleting Blog.* https://blog.efpsa.org/2018/01/03/writing-a-systematic-literature-review/

Tan, K. (2013). A framework for assessment for learning: implications for feedback practices within and beyond the gap. *International Scholarly Research Notices, 2013, 1-6*. https://doi.org/10.1155/2013/640609

Vassiliou, S., & Papadima-Sophocleous, S. (2019). A systematic review and annotated bibliography of second language learning formative assessment: an overview. *Conference Proceedings, 12th International Conference Innovation in Language Learning* (pp. 352-362). https://conference.pixel-online.net/ICT4LL/files/ict4ll/ed0012/Conference%20Proceedings.pdf

Wang, T.-H. (2008). Web-based quiz-game-like formative assessment: development and evaluation. *Computers & Education, 51*(3), 1247-1263. https://doi.org/10.1016/j.compedu.2007.11.011

Wiliam, D. (2011). What is assessment for learning? *Studies In Educational Evaluation, 37*(1), 3-14. https://doi.org/10.1016/j.stueduc.2011.03.001

When teachers do Formative Assessment effectively, students learn at roughly double the rate than they do without it.

Dylan Wiliam

PART 2

A systematic review of formative assessment in language learning

2.1. Introduction

A Systematic Review (SR) is "the art and science of identifying, selecting, and [synthesising] primary research studies to provide a comprehensive and trustworthy picture of the topic being studied" (Oakley, 2012, cited in Crompton, Burke, & Gregory, 2017, p. 5). According to Crompton, Burke, and Lin (2019), an SR "can uncover new trends and additional findings" (p. 5). In the case of Formative Assessment (FA) research, scholars aggregate findings to gain a better understanding of how FA is supporting Language Learning (LL) (Bachelor & Bachelor, 2016; Graham, Harris, & Hebert, 2011; Jian & Luo, 2014; Saoud, 2016; Widiastuti & Saukah, 2017; Wolf, Shore, & Blood, 2014).

With more and more frequent use of FA in LL, and as stated by Crompton et al. (2017), "it is critical to maintain an updated synthesised collection of research so that the scholarly community can remain current in their understanding of [FA] and its impact on student learning. Furthermore, it is of [great importance] that researchers continue to add to this growing base of scholarly knowledge by investigating unexamined or under-examined questions surrounding [FA in LL]" (p. 1), such as the type of publications in the researched period of time, the research purposes and types, the research designs, methods, and data collection tools and expected outcomes of these studies; the languages, the types of participants, and the education levels (primary, secondary, tertiary) in the publications studied; the types of FA applications used in LL in the research studied; the focus of the LL; the learning theories and teaching methods supporting the FA LL researched; and the major geographic distribution in the studies of FA in LL.

Based on this rationale, and on the fact that there is a gap in the area of SR in FA in LL since the beginning of FA in LL, the purpose of this SR is to deliver the scholarly community with a current sum of evidence and a synthesis of FA in LL research conducted in the period of 20 years (2000-2020). It aims to offer an analysis of the specific LL FA practices by answering specific research questions and suggesting further research in the area. In order to have an overview of the main characteristics of the studies involving FA in LL from 2000 to 2020, this SR was guided by the below tentative research questions.

- What were the major publication types, research purposes, research design types, methods, data collection tools, and outcomes?

- What were the languages, participant types, and educational levels involved in the studies?

- Which types of FA applications were used in LL research studies?

- Which was the LL focus formatively assessed?

- What learning theories and language teaching methods were used to support FA in LL?

- What was the geographic distribution of LL FA studies?

These tentative research questions framed eight features that were identified for analysis as it was conducted in other SRs and used as predetermined codes for the qualitative analysis (Crompton et al., 2019; Spolaôr & Benitti, 2017). These main categories/codes were the following.

- *Publication type*: the types of publications were classified as scientific peer-reviewed: journal articles, conference proceedings papers, short papers, book chapters, books, handbooks, doctoral or master theses, or reports.

- *Research type:* the research type aimed to identify the main research designs, methodologies (e.g. qualitative, quantitative, mixed; case study, action research, etc.), and data collection tools that were applied in FA in LL studies.

- *Research purpose and outcomes*: this category aimed to identify the main purpose and outcomes of the publications reviewed.

- *The language(s) studied, participant types and educational level*: another category aimed to identify, establish, and record (1) the languages explored in research in FA in LL; (2) the types of participants (students, teachers, or both) in the research under examination; and (3) the level of educational studies (primary, secondary, and tertiary) FA in LL research was carried out for, and the potential research gaps in specific educational levels.

- *FA types*: this category aimed to investigate and record the most commonly used types of FA applied in LL.

- *Language focus*: this classification aimed to bring light into the LL focus of the FA in LL research carried out.

- *Learning theories and language teaching methods:* this category aimed to record the learning theories supporting the use of FA in LL.

- *Geographic distribution of the use of FA in LL studies*: this categorisation aimed to provide a chart of the countries where the studies took place and demonstrate the activity on FA in LL at country level worldwide.

2.2. Methodology

This book focused on the years 2000 (Rea-Dickins & Gardner, 2000: first publication referring to FA in LL) to 2020. Searches included scientific reviewed publications written in English and published between 2000 and 2020.

2.2.1. How the literature search was conducted

This SR is informed by methodology procedures followed in other SR (e.g. Crompton et al., 2019; Poole & Clarke-Midura, 2020; Spolaôr & Benitti, 2017). The SR follows a qualitative research method in order to summarise the studies conducted on the subject. During the search, particular sections of the publications were looked at in order to inform the selection process. These sections were looked at in the following order: titles, abstract, table of contents, whole text. If the title was relevant to the topic, the abstract was looked at, and then the rest of the aspects. If one of the aspects was irrelevant, the publication was not considered for this review.

An initial search was conducted in electronic databases. The following table presents the electronic databases and electronic resources that were used for the purpose of this research.

Table 2.1. Databases used in SRs

Bibliographic databases	Database URL
EBSCOhost	http://web.a.ebscohost.com
ERIC	https://eric.ed.gov/
ResearchGate	https://www.researchgate.net/
Google Scholar	https://scholar.google.com/

The study selection consisted of applying search strings from the above bibliographical databases described (Table 2.1). The search included strings such as below.

- (Formative Assessment) AND (Second Language Teaching) OR (Second Language Learning)

- (Classroom Assessment) AND (Second Language Teaching) OR (Second Language Learning)

- (Alternative Assessment) AND (Second Language Teaching) OR (Second Language Learning)

- (Portfolio Assessment) AND (Second Language Teaching) OR (Second Language Learning)

2.2.2. Inclusion/exclusion criteria

After a close study of SR inclusion/exclusion criteria (Meline, 2006; Piper, 2013; Saldaña, 2015; The University of Melbourne, 2021), a number of criteria were specified to select studies for inclusion in the review. The following 12 criteria were used to determine which types of publications to include in the review:

- the publication was published between 2000-2020;

- the publication was peer-reviewed (journal articles, conference proceedings papers, short papers, book chapters, books, handbooks, Doctoral or Master theses, research reports);

- the publisher or type of publication (journal, book, etc.) where the research was found is distinguished and reviewed by professionals in the field;

- the publication included at least two of the search terms;

- the publication matched the predetermined characteristics used in other SR and served the purposes of this SR;

- author(s) had credibility with institutional affiliation, educational background, past writing experience as it relates to research, or text written in the author's area of expertise, and the author has been cited in other sources or bibliographies;

- the publication reported the application of FA in LL;

- the information is verified in another source or the author gives evidence to their findings;

- the publication presented FA in LL in a primary, secondary, or tertiary context;

- the publication presented a quantitative or a qualitative or a mixed research approach to researching FA in LL;

- the publication was well written; and

- the publication contributed to the aim of this book, which is to give an overview of the activity in L2 FA in the last 20 years.

Seven criteria for exclusion of articles were also identified:

- the publication was not published between 2000-2020;

- the publication did not match the predetermined characteristics, and emerging code used in other SRs, and did not serve the purposes of this SR;

- the publication was hosted in web pages that are not freely accessed and only abstracts were accessed;

- the publication is composed of only one page (abstract papers), posters, scientific events programmes, and tutorial slides;

- the publication duplicated other publications by the same author (similar title, abstract, results, or text). In such a case, only one was included in this review;

- the publication's writing style did not meet academic expectations; and

- the publication was written in a language other than English.

As mentioned earlier, studies considered for inclusion within the SR were first identified from titles and abstracts generated from one of two sources: electronic databases, and other electronic resources. The study search was applied for work published between 2000-2020 using the electronic databases presented in Table 2.1. As a result, a total number of 16,475 research publications were identified. The number was considerably decreased to 104 after applying the inclusion/exclusion criteria. Table 2.2 presents the number of publications that were found in each electronic database before and after applying the inclusion/exclusion criteria.

Table 2.2. Number of papers before and after the inclusion/exclusion criteria

Database	Frequency	
	Initial Search	After the inclusion/exclusion criteria
EBSCOhost	151	11
ERIC	351	19
Google Scholar	15,721	57
Research Gate	252	16

Most of the publications were found via Google Scholar (57.44%) and ERIC (16.49%) databases. The exclusion criteria significantly decreased the number of documents that were related to the use of FA in LL.

An initial search in databases resulted in 16,475 papers. The first exclusion criterion eliminated 5,828 publications, as they were not published in the chronological period 2000-2020; 10,647 publications remained. With the second

Part 2

criterion, 4,375 were removed since they dealt with FA generically and were not related to the use of FA in LL. The third exclusion criterion eliminated 2,861 publications since they were not freely accessed and only abstracts could be accessed by the researcher. The remaining 3,590 studies were further evaluated to ensure that they fulfilled the other inclusion/exclusion criteria. Another 1,305 studies were also removed according to the fourth exclusion criterion, since they were composed only of one page. The fifth exclusion criterion eliminated another 1,409 publications since they were duplicated. Moreover, according to the sixth criterion, 593 publications were removed since they were written in languages other than English. The search process is presented in Figure 2.1.

Figure 2.1. The search strategy and review process

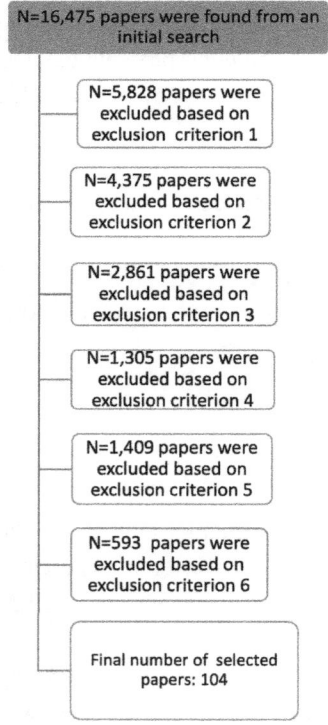

The 104 papers that were included in the SR and AB met all the inclusion criteria.

2.2.3. Coding

Once the selection of the publications was completed with the use of the set of inclusion/exclusion criteria, and a specific number of publications was determined, methodology procedures used in SRs were explored in order to analyse the data. As SRs mainly follow a qualitative research method, a study of coding procedures was carried out to decide on the ones that would best suit this SR. According to Creswell (2009, p. 187), there are three approaches to coding:

- developing codes only on the basis of the emerging information collected from participants;

- using predetermined codes and then fitting the data to them; or

- using some combination of predetermined and emerging code.

The combination of the predetermined and emerging code approach was followed to collect and analyse the data. A deductive coding or a concept-driven approach with code themes was first applied. These code themes were predefined by the researchers based on the inclusion and exclusion criteria (Medelyan, 2020). During the coding procedure, however, other interesting themes emerged. These were also recorded and analysed.

Data were analysed by following a coding process, which is a procedure of analysing qualitative inquiries; it is a way of mapping or tagging data that are related to a particular research question (Elliott, 2018; Saldaña, 2015). Qualitative data were then graphed in various ways, e.g. using figures (Qualitative Variables, 2009). Such figures are used in order to identify percentages of the themes identified.

Part 2

2.2.4. Analysis framework

The coding enabled the researchers to obtain concrete data, in order to better synthesise and interpret the results. The data examination and analysis also helped in refining and improving the original research questions. Moreover, it enabled the researchers to evaluate and compare the data and come to some new suggestions and recommendations for future research (Saldaña, 2015).

2.3. Results

One hundred and four (104) publications were screened, assessed for eligibility by the three SR authors, and included in this review. This process was carried out from 2019 to February 2022. The analysis of the data helped finalise the formation of the research questions. Some substantial considerations and conclusions about the implementation of FA in LL were noted, based on the research questions and the data analysis. The following is a description of the results.

2.3.1. Major types of publications, research purposes, research types, methods, data collection tools, and outcomes identified in the studies involving FA in LL

2.3.1.1. Type of publications

The following figure presents the types of publications for FA in LL from 2000 to 2020 included in the SR (Figure 2.2).

The majority of publications were research articles with a percentage of 80%, followed by book chapters with 3%, Master dissertations with 3%, conference papers with 3%, reports with 3%, short papers with 3%, books with 2%, Doctoral dissertations with 2%, and symposium papers with 1%.

Figure 2.2. Types of publications in FA in LL practices

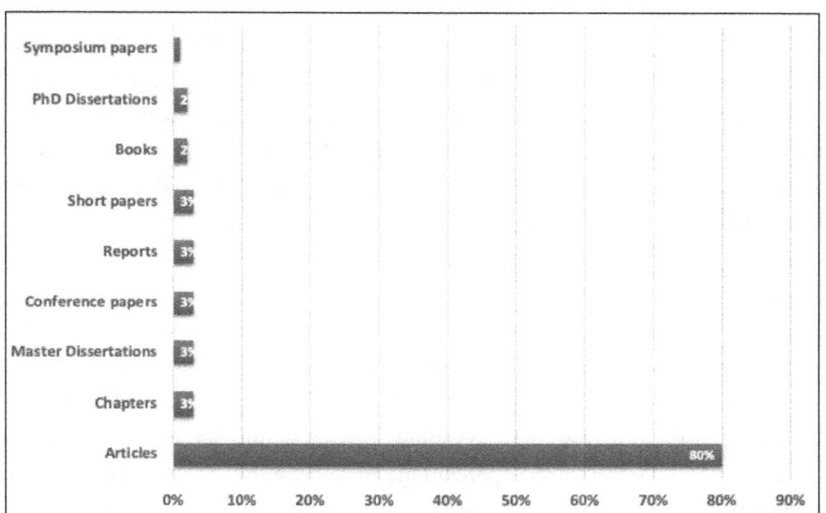

2.3.1.2. Research purposes

A large number of research studies up to 97% aimed to investigate or collect data about the use of FA in learning and teaching a L2. The rest included literature reviews or other publications. More specifically, 35% of them aimed to display the important role of providing feedback to students which is the core characteristic of FA (Bachelor & Bachelor, 2016; Bahati, Tedre, Fors, & Evode, 2016; Burner, 2016; Chen, May, Klenowski, & Kettle, 2014; Fakeye, 2016; Levy & Gertler, 2015; Titova, 2015; Tsagari & Michaeloudes, 2013). Also, 24% of the studies sought to identify if PA for FA purposes is considered effective for L2 learning and teaching (Burner, 2014, 2016; Cummins & Davesne, 2009; Little, 2002; Papadima-Sophocleous, 2017; Phung, 2016; Rezaee, Alavi, & Shabani, 2013). Furthermore, 14% of studies investigated the different types of assessment practices of L2 instructors in different countries (Leung & Rea-Dickins, 2007); 10% of the publications discussed that, although there is interest globally in FA in LL and is applied in many cases, there was still a dominance of test-driven formal assessment environments in many countries and that these caused stress and anxiety to students (Leung & Rea-Dickins, 2007; Rea-Dickins, 2004; Tsagari, 2004). Additionally, a significant number of 7% of publications aimed to identify if students were trained in FA practices. Furthermore, 10% revealed that researchers, on the one hand, seek to discover if the integration of digital tools enables teachers to introduce better FA practices, and on the other hand, if students accept and better understand the importance of FA through digital applications.

2.3.1.3. Research types

Research types were identified by taking into consideration the research designs reported in the sources examined. They have been recorded and coded as mentioned in the publications. The major research type, as indicated from the data analysis, is 'study' with a percentage of 42%, either mentioned as a study or comparative study, case study, or pilot study. For that reason, the authors have investigated the research methodologies and research tools that were mentioned in the publications in-depth so as to collect more information about the type of study. However, the only information for the research type or design that was mentioned was the word 'study'. The percentage of research papers mentioned only as a study is about 22%, followed by a case study with 8.25%, a comparative study with a percentage of 6.25%, and a pilot study with a percentage of 5.5%. This also happened with the use of the word 'research'. Twenty per cent (20%) were described as only 'research' with no further indication as to what type of research it was in each case, 'survey' was represented with a percentage of 12.4%, 'action research' with a percentage of 8.8%, 'literature review' with a percentage of 7%, 'exploratory analysis' with a percentage of 2.7%, 'experiment project' with 2%, 'review' with 3.2%, and 'systematic review' with 1.9%. The main characteristic of the types of sources investigated that used study research design (either as a case study or comparative study or pilot study) were interviews and observations to identify the impact of language FA integrations into their classes. Overall, eight different research types were reported. Table 2.3 presents the major research types that were applied in FA in LL publications, as reported in the publications.

Table 2.3. Major research designs that were used for FA in LL practices

Study	42%
Research	20%
Survey	12.4%
Action Research	8.8%
Literature Review	7%
Review	3.2%
Exploratory Analysis	2.7%
Experiment Project	2%
Systematic Review	1.9%

This data analysis revealed that the majority of research publications did not clearly state their type of research: 42% of the publications did not clearly indicate what type of study/research the publication was. Twenty-two per cent of publications were mentioned as just study and 20% as just research. The rest of them clearly stated what type of research they were ('survey' 12.4%, 'action research' 8.8%, 'literature review' 7%, 'review' 3.2%, 'exploratory analysis' 2.7%, 'experiment project' 2%, and 'systematic review' 1.9%).

2.3.1.4. Research methods and data collection tools

The dominant research method that was applied by researchers FA in LL, as extracted from the data, is the qualitative method with a percentage of 39.4%, followed by the quantitative method with a percentage of 32.4%, and the mixed method with 28.2%. Moreover, it seems that the most common research tool that was applied by researchers was interviews with a percentage of 29%, followed by questionnaires with 24%, observations with 20%, pre-post tests with 17%, video-audio recordings with 6%, transcripts of students' work with 4%.

2.3.1.5. Research outcomes

The outcomes of the research publications examined included the impact of FA application to both teachers and students.

Part 2

A total of 95% publications reported a positive impact of FA in LL practices on students' motivation and progress. A low 3.7% did not mention any impact of FA in LL practices on students or teachers. Moreover, it has been stated that the positive impact of FA on students may increase cooperative learning by integrating peer assessment (Hansson, 2015).

Another theme that emerged from the qualitative data analysis in some research papers was that of reduction of students' anxiety (Bayat, Jamshidipour, & Hashemi, 2017; Ketabi & Ketabi, 2014; Tang, 2016). It has been noted that FA practices and multimedia tools can reduce students' anxiety and improve oral performance (Tang, 2016). Also, in Bayat et al. (2017) it was concluded that formative quizzes can also reduce students' anxiety and improve their listening skills.

In 19% of the publications, it was stated that teachers had a positive attitude towards using FA in their practice. Some studies focused on specific FA aspects which had a negative effect, for example, in some cases it has been argued that portfolios used for FA purposes are time-consuming for students (Guadu & Boersma, 2018). They have been considered time-consuming as well for teachers to provide feedback, especially in classes with a big number of students (Tsagari, 2004).

Furthermore, a number of studies have highlighted the fact that the educational system was still largely based on formal traditional testing assessment and there were fewer cases where alternative types of assessment were implemented (Rezaee et al., 2013). Additionally, in other studies, it has been argued that language teachers still preferred using summative based testing assessment tasks due to the belief that SA provides them with a clearer picture of their students' performances (Tsagari, 2016).

In addition, some other publications have indicated that there are some significant considerations regarding the lack of teachers' knowledge and training in LAL (Crusan et al., 2016; Lam, 2015; Tsagari & Michaeloudes, 2013; Tsagari et al., 2018). Numerous studies have concluded that pre-service and in-service L2 teachers need specific training in LAL in implementing FA practices and their level in LAL was low (Crusan et al., 2016; Lam, 2015; Tsagari & Michaeloudes, 2013).

2.3.2. Languages, types of participants, and educational levels in the publications studied, involving FA in LL

2.3.2.1. Languages

Figure 2.3 indicates that the dominant language in LL FA research, which was conducted in English, was for EFL/ESL. This was reflected in 84% of the research publications. Then, it was followed by research for EAL with 6%, for Spanish with 3%, French with 3%, Italian with 3%, and Sign Language as an L2 with 1%.

Figure 2.3. Languages in FA in LL applications

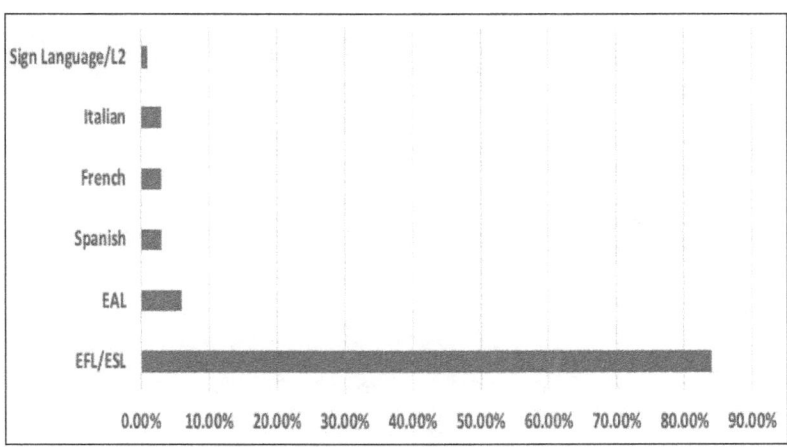

2.3.2.2. Types of participants

Another theme that emerged from the data was the type and number of participants who took part in the various research projects. It is clear from the information presented in Figure 2.4 that the majority of the studies were carried out with participants as students, with a percentage of 45%; then as teachers, with a percentage of 37%, followed by both teachers and students with a percentage of 18%.

Figure 2.4. Participants in LL FA research implementations

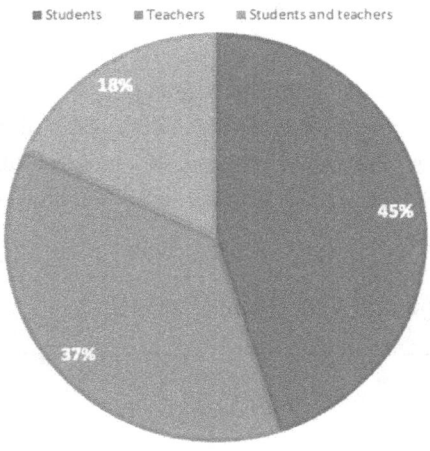

2.3.2.3. Types of educational levels

Figure 2.5 clearly indicates that the majority of research for FA practices has been carried out at the tertiary level with 62%, at the secondary level with 18%, and at primary level with 20%.

Figure 2.5. Language FA practices at different educational levels

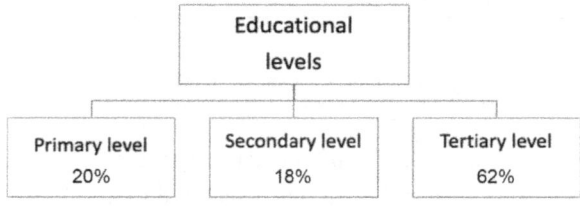

The data reveal that tertiary settings were the most frequent. Therefore, it is evident that college and university students and teachers as participants experienced the most language FA practices compared to primary and secondary education students and teachers.

2.3.2.4. Types of FA applications in LL studies

The information in Figure 2.6 displays the types of activities used as FAs in LL that were reported in the investigated publications.

Figure 2.6. Types of FAs used in LL

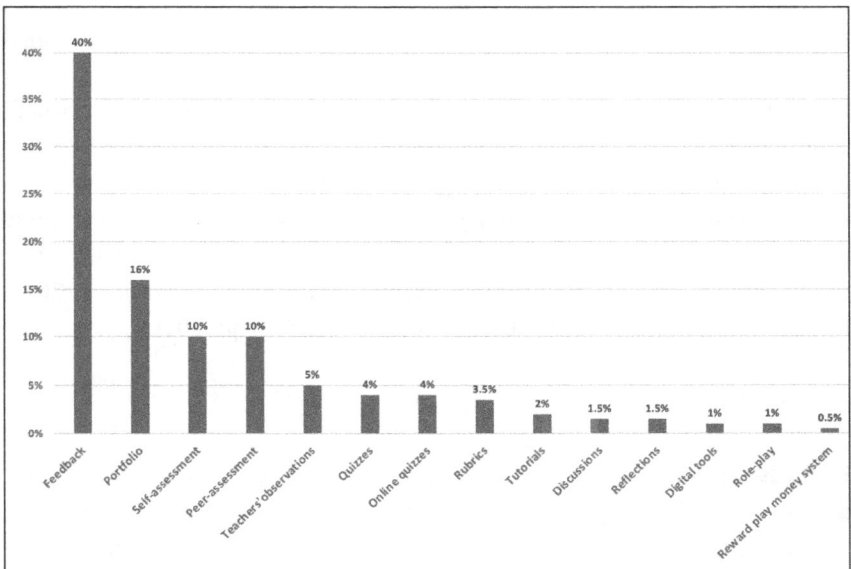

The most frequently reported was the provision of feedback with 40%. Feedback was reported in papers as 'corrective feedback', 'online feedback', 'peer feedback', 'diagnostic feedback', 'audio feedback' and 'criterion feedback'. The portfolio was next in frequency with 16%, followed by self-assessment with 10%, then peer assessment with 10%, reflections with 1.5%, quizzes with 3%, online quizzes (Socrative, Kahoot, Edmodo, Padlet, Storify, Quizlet) with 3%, rubrics with 3.5%, teachers' observations with 5%, tutorials with 2%, discussions with 1.5%, digital tools (iPods and iPads) with 1%, role-play with 1%, and reward play money systems with 1%. It is worth mentioning that technology-enhanced activities are gaining ground in LL FA (Cummins & Davesne, 2009; Levy & Gertler, 2015; Pinto-Llorente, Sánchez-Gómez, García-Peñalvo, & Martín, 2016; Saglam, 2018).

The information collected from the qualitative analysis of the data about FA types in LL also indicates the significant role of digital tools in LL FA practices; 25.65% of the FA types involved digital tools or applications that were used by teachers. These included online quizzes (Socrative, Kahoot, Edmodo, Padlet, Storify, Quizlet) with 5.5%, online portfolios with 7%, and digital tools (iPods and iPads) with 0.9%. Moreover, online feedback was used by either the teacher or by a peer (12.25%). Also, it is stated that learners benefit from receiving computer formative feedback and their speaking and writing skills improve (Levy & Gertler, 2015). Learners are benefitted from the instant feedback and the positive environment that digital tools offer. The game-based characteristic of these digital tools can enhance their language skills according to the findings from the publications examined (Cummins & Davesne, 2009; Levy & Gertler, 2015; Pinto-Llorente et al., 2016; Saglam, 2018).

2.3.2.5. FA LL focus

Language teaching, learning, and assessment have a long history since ancient times. The focus depended on the reasons people learned a language. According to Howatt and Smith's (2014) synoptic overview, modern language teaching in Europe included the following periods: the Classical Period (1750-1880), which focused on emulating the teaching of classical languages (based on the model of teaching Latin and Greek), and was associated with grammar-translation and classical methods of teaching; the Reform Period (1880-1920), which focused on teaching the spoken language and was associated with various reform methods such as the natural method, the berlitz methods and the direct method; the Scientific Period (1920-1970), which focused on a scientific basis for teaching and was associated with teaching methods such as the oral method, the multiple line of approach, the situational approach, the oral approach and the audiolingual method; the Communicative Period (1970-2000+), which aimed to teach for 'real-life' communication and was associated with communicative language teaching and task-based language teaching methods. One can notice through the study of these periods, that the focus changed direction from the traditional language teaching coverage of specific language skills such as reading, speaking, listening, and writing and language aspects such as grammar and vocabulary to a more integrative way of dealing with all these for 'real life' communication. One of the aims of this review was to identify the focus of the research conducted in the area of FA in LL in the period 2000-2020, in other words, to find out whether it followed this trend. Figure 2.7 displays the percentages of the focus of these publications.

Figure 2.7. Language focus of FA in LL

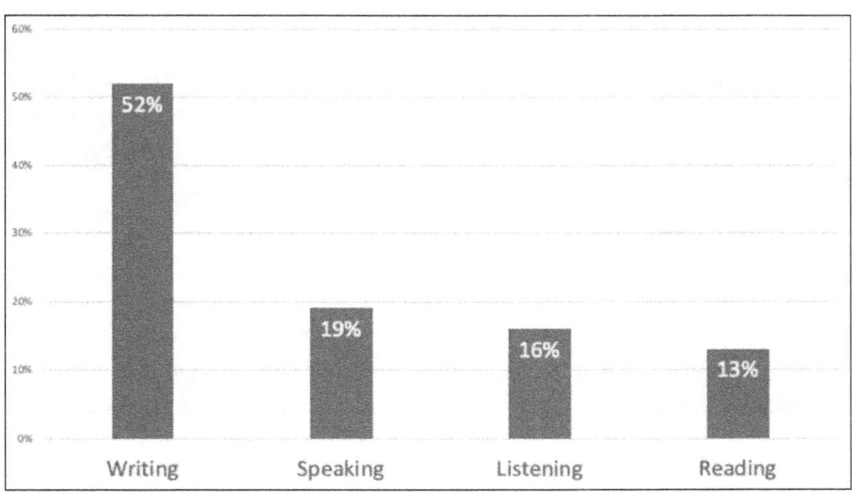

According to the data shown in Figure 2.7, most FA in LL research publications were carried out for writing skills with 52%. Oral communication skills come second with 19%, then listening skills with 16%, and reading with 13%.

According to the publications examined, most of the research on FA for writing skills was implemented in an academic writing environment (65%) and 35% at the secondary educational level. The most common tool that was used for writing skills for FA purposes was the portfolio as it was considered as alternative evidence of students' writing performance (Burner, 2014; Cummins & Davesne, 2009; Lam, 2015; Little, 2002; Papadima-Sophocleous, 2017; Phung, 2016; Rezaee et al., 2013). Other tools that were used to assess writing skills formatively were blogs, peer- and self-feedback, AWE tools, and journals.

For speaking communication skills, 60% of the research has been carried out at the tertiary level; 25% in primary educational settings, and 15% in secondary educational settings.

For listening skills, 55% of the studies have been carried out in tertiary settings, 25% in secondary settings, and 20% in primary settings. The most frequent tools used to formatively assess listening were iPods, iPads, online quizzes, and portfolios.

According to the publications examined, most of the research on FA for reading skills was carried out at the tertiary level as well (68%) followed by 32% at the secondary educational level. Some of the tools used to formatively assess reading skills were ELFA and portfolios.

2.3.2.6. Language aspects

Most publications on FA in LL treated either language skills or other aspects (72%). Vocabulary was mentioned in 8% of the studies and grammar in 4%. Many publications mentioned the role of gamified quizzes for the acquisition of L2 vocabulary and grammar and the increase of students' performance with a percentage of 15.6% (Pinto-Llorente et al., 2016). The significant role of feedback in the acquisition of vocabulary was also highlighted (Titova, 2015). It is worth mentioning that in some educational systems, more emphasis is put on assessing grammar and vocabulary than on language skills (Tsagari, 2016). Some particular software like Grammarly and Turnitin Quickmark were recorded as tools that provide opportunities for electronic feedback in grammar, vocabulary, and pronunciation (Williamson & Sadera, 2016).

2.3.2.7. Other aspects: gender, student anxiety reduction

Another aspect that has been noted during the data analysis was that participants in almost all of the studies presented so far were both male and female, with the exception of only one case, where participants were only females (Chen et al., 2013).

Another theme that emerged from the qualitative data analysis in some research papers was that of reduction of students' anxiety (Bayat et al., 2017; Ketabi & Ketabi, 2014; Tang, 2016). Researchers noted that FA practices and multimedia tools used reduce students' anxiety and improve oral performance (Tang, 2016). Also, Chen et al. (2013) have argued that participants from an urban and regional university in China shared the same understanding of FA, in addition to differences which are related to their sociocultural conditions, beliefs on teachers' and students' roles, and expectations in English.

2.3.3. Learning theories and teaching methods used to support FA in LL

LL, teaching, and assessment are based on some teaching approach or method, which is based on some learning theory. Very often, in our teacher training programmes, we noticed that language practitioners tend to base their teaching more on practice and are often not clear of the learning theory and teaching methods their teaching is based on. For this reason, the publications were also reviewed to explore this aspect in the research carried out on FA in LL. The data analysis revealed that only a small number of studies (4.8%) mentioned the learning theories, learning approaches and learning methods that support the concept of the use of FA in teaching and learning (Chen & Zhang, 2017; Davison, 2019; Kuo, 2015; Little, 2002; Poehner & Lantolf, 2005). The dominant learning theory, as found in 2% of the publications, that supports FA practices in L2 environments is Vygotsky's sociocultural theory of learning. According to

Part 2

Vygotsky, learning occurs as a result of interaction with others where alternative types of assessment are suggested (Poehner & Lantolf, 2005). Moreover, another important language theory mentioned is the constructivism theory of learning, where students have an active involvement in their learning and in their own assessment with a percentage of 1.5% (Buyukkarci, 2010). Additionally, a process-oriented approach was mentioned in one paper. According to this approach, the learner practices writing skills for authentic purposes and the whole procedure includes pre-writing, writing, revising, editing and sharing (Kuo, 2015).

2.3.4. Major geographic distributions in studies involving FA in LL

This SR also investigated the geographic distribution of research in the use of FA in LL practices. The aim of this was to establish the current research practices in FA in LL and identify possible needs and themes that may need to be further researched in the future. Location is related to where research was conducted. If the publication was not related to a research paper, the location of the researcher's affiliation was recorded as '*location*'.

The SR reveals that studies took place in all continents except Antarctica. It was found that the continent with the highest percentage was Asia with a percentage of 40%, followed by Europe with 25%, America (South and North) with 22%, Oceania with 10%, and Africa with 3%. The data showed that Asia is the most active continent, with China and Iran presenting 19% of the total amount of publications (Figure 2.8).

Within these continents, a total number of 39 countries were represented. From Figure 2.9, it is evident that the US has the highest percentage (18%) of studies in the use of FA in LL, followed by China with 10%, Iran with 9%, Turkey with 8%, Australia with 8%, Norway with 5%, the UK with 5%, Canada with 4%, Taiwan with 3.5%, Cyprus with 3%, Malaysia with 3%, Japan, Canada, New Zealand with 2% each, and South Korea, Spain, Greece, Indonesia, Thailand, Colombia, Ethiopia, Chile, Israel, Italy, Nigeria, Netherlands, and Russia with

1% each. The significance of these findings is elaborated further on in the discussion section.

Figure 2.8. Geographic distribution of FA in LL in continents

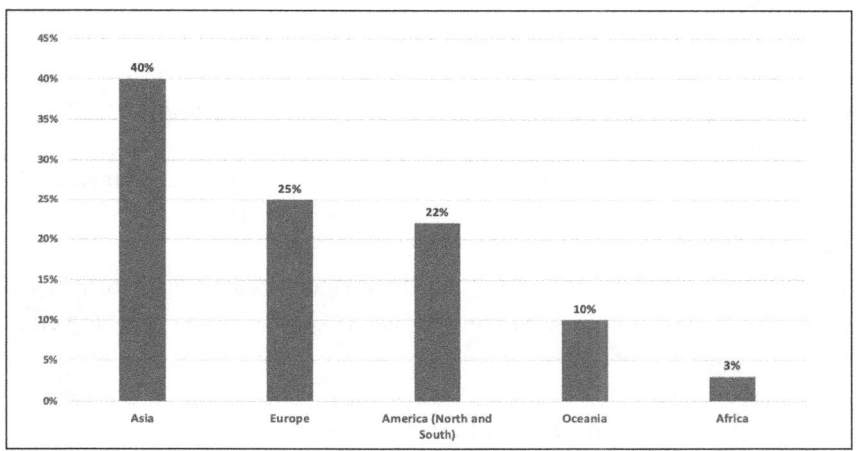

Figure 2.9. Geographic distribution of the use of FA in LL in countries

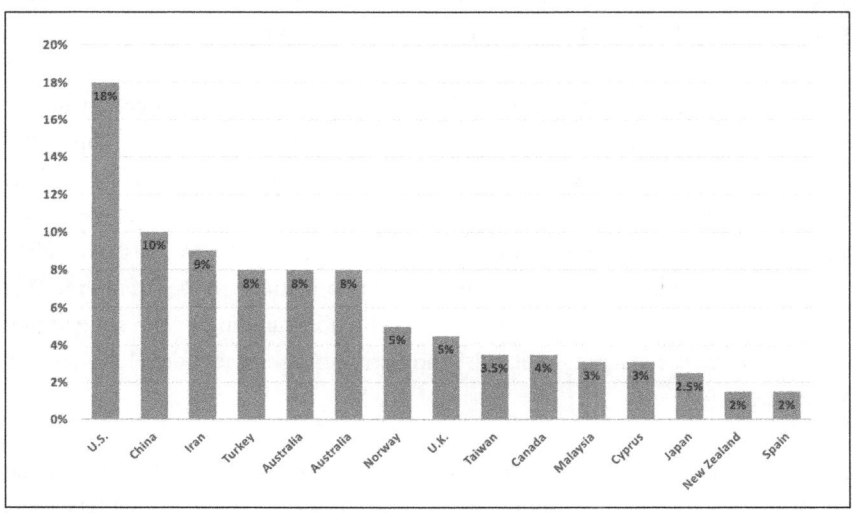

Part 2

The findings of this SR reveal a global interest in the use of FA in LL, and the distribution of this interest (Figure 2.8 and Figure 2.9).

2.4. Discussion

The combination of predetermined and emerging code approaches used for the collection of the data (Creswell, 2009) was also used for the qualitative analysis and discussion of the results. The analysis and discussion evolved around the research questions and the eight features that were identified (Crompton et al., 2019; Spolaôr & Benitti, 2017), as well as the emerged themes.

The SR of these 104 publications and the method used brought to light the following insights related to research in FA in LL during the specific period under review.

2.4.1. The increasing interest in the use of FA in LL in recent years

The data analysis revealed that FA is gaining ground in LL research in recent years. Figure 2.10 illustrates the number of publications per year.

According to the literature, during the first attempts of FA application in LL, between 2000 to 2011, there was somewhat low activity in the area. This is not surprising as stakeholders need some time to get used to new concepts such as FA, and engage in its application and research. During the next half of the period examined, the data reveal a growing interest, with the years 2016 and 2017 recording contributing the largest number of publications to the literature. This can be attributed to the increase in the holders' understanding of current learning theories, language teaching methods, and deriving assessment development and applications.

The availability of digital tools in LL may have also offered additional opportunities, for example, digital tools can contribute to giving instant feedback, and online FA tools can improve students' language skills (Pinto-Llorente et al., 2016; Williamson & Sadera, 2016). The implementation of technology enables teachers to collect data during lessons from students' performances and helps them to assess their progress on a continuous basis (Joyce, 2018; Levy & Gertler, 2015; Pinto-Llorente et al., 2016; Williamson & Sadera, 2016).

Figure 2.10. Number of publications in each year the use of FA practices in LL

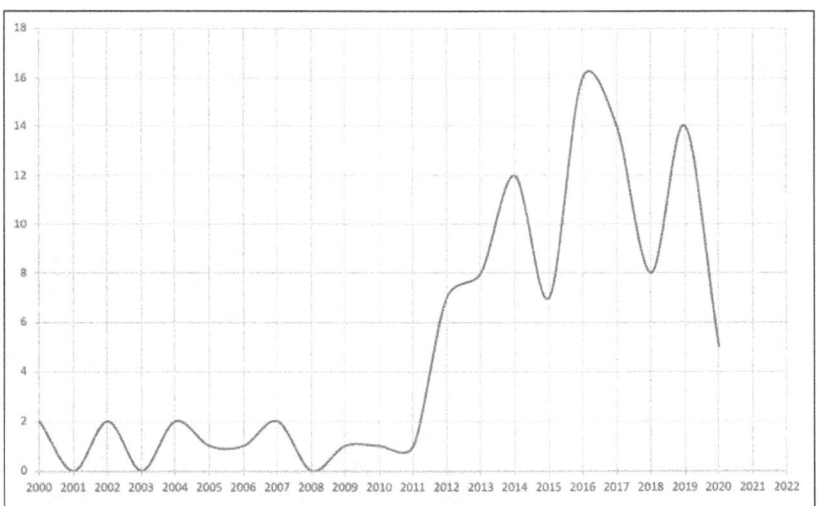

2.4.2. Types of publications

The findings revealed that from 2000 to 2020, the types of publications that were published were mostly articles (80%). This reveals the interest in research in this area and the urge of researchers to inform and share such research with the FA in LL research community and other stakeholders in recognised scientific publications. The rest (books, book chapters, reviewed conference papers, doctoral and Master dissertations to short papers and reports) were less than 5%. The number of publications in the form of scientific and reviewed books and book chapters indicate that researchers may need to be encouraged to engage more in such activity in this form. More research by postgraduate students at

Part 2

MA and PhD level is also recorded to be needed (Buyukkarci, 2010; Kuo, 2015; Meissner, 2018; Radford, 2014; Saoud, 2016; Vågen, 2017). This book may prove to be useful to those interested in the different types of publications, their value and characteristics, and work as a guide as to what form of research has been conducted and what needs to be further researched.

2.4.3. Research purposes

The examination of the data regarding the purposes of the research publications revealed that these evolved around the following topics: (1) the importance of the role of providing feedback to students (Bachelor & Bachelor, 2016; Bahati et al., 2016; Burner, 2016; Chen et al., 2014; Fakeye, 2016; Levy & Gertler, 2015; Titova, 2015; Tsagari & Michaeloudes, 2013), (2) the identification of the effectiveness of PA for L2 learning and teaching (Burner, 2014, 2016; Crusan et al., 2016; Cummins & Davesne, 2009; Little, 2002; Papadima-Sophocleous, 2017; Phung, 2016; Radford, 2014; Rezaee et al., 2013), (3) the identification of the different types of assessment practices in different countries (Leung & Rea-Dickins, 2007), (4) the fact that 10% of the publications discussed that there was still a dominance of test-driven formal assessment environments, (5) the extent of test-driven formal assessment environments in many countries and their cause of stress and anxiety to students even though FA applications are being used (Crusan et al., 2016; Leung & Rea-Dickins, 2007; Phung, 2016; Radford, 2014; Rea-Dickins, 2004; Tsagari, 2004), (6) the identification of student training in FA in LL practices, (7) the identification of the role of technologies in the introduction of better FA practices by the teachers, and (8) the acceptance and better understanding from students of the importance of FA through digital applications. Although the data analysis made a number of FA in LL research purposes known, it also revealed that there are a lot of FA in LL research purposes that need further examination or have not yet been examined, areas such as a clearer definition of formative assessment, a clearer understanding of formative and summative assessments and the way some assessments are used differently for formative or summative assessment purposes, the distance between FA in LL policies, and their actual application during the learning process, etc.

2.4.4. Research types

A close look at the types of research identified in the 104 publications reviewed confirms that the majority tends not to clearly state the types of study/research the publications are based on. For example, where in some cases it is clearly stated that it is a case study or a pilot study, in many others it is referred to only with the word 'study'. This may suggest that the authors may not think it is important to mention what type their research is, or they may not be clear on their research type. The results can also suggest that this phenomenon has not been much researched. The lack of such reference in earlier research is indicative. This could be a focus of future studies.

2.4.5. Research methods and data collection tools

The qualitative method was most practised with a percentage of 39.4%, (Bahati et al., 2016; Guadu & Boersma, 2018; Haines, Meima, & Faber, 2013; Lam, 2015; Rezaee et al., 2013; Saliu Abdulahi, 2017; Vågen, 2017; Widiastuti, Mukminatien, Prayogo, & Irawati, 2020), followed by the quantitative method with a percentage of 32.4% (Caruso, Gadd Colombi, & Tebbit, 2017; Pinto-Llorente et al., 2016; Seyyedrezaie, Ghansoli, Shahriari, & Fatemi, 2016), and the mixed method with a percentage of 28.2% (Chen & Zhang, 2017; Cotter & Hinkelman, 2019; Guadu & Boersma, 2018; Naghdipour, 2017; Tang, 2016; Tsagari & Michaeloudes, 2013; Yarahmadzehi & Goodarzi, 2020). Some common research outcomes emerged from the qualitative data analysis of the types of sources examined. These findings established that all three methods were nearly equally used. Furthermore, the types of research methods used in these publications reflect a balanced application of all three. It seems that collecting data through qualitative research tools was preferable to many researchers. However, the great number of papers with a mixed method approach, where researchers combine qualitative and quantitative data cannot be ignored, as their outcomes are considered more valid and offer a deeper and clearer understanding of the findings (McKim, 2017).

The examination of data collection tools also recorded the use of a variety ranging from interviews, questionnaires, observations, pre- and post-tests, video-audio recordings, and transcripts of students' work. The findings also revealed a widespread use of these tools by many researchers. Future research may focus on the quality of the use of these research methods and tools.

2.4.6. Research outcomes

The outcomes of the research publications under examination affirmed mostly a positive impact of FA in LL (Bayat et al., 2017; Caruso et al., 2017; Chen & Zhang, 2017; Fakeye, 2016; Naghdipour, 2017). This is a good finding as it may encourage teachers reluctant to integrate FA in their teaching to do so. The majority of the studies also suggested that the integration of FA for learning an L2/FL may increase students' motivation, and as a result improve of their LL (Alzaid & Alkarzae, 2019; Ammar, 2020; Vassiliou & Papadima-Sophocleous, 2019). It may also enable teachers to collect more data and information about their students' progress, and use it to improve the learning process (Huang, 2016; Little, 2002; Smith & Davis, 2014).

In the publications examined, the use of assessment activities for FA purposes such as peer assessment creates a more comforting feeling to students towards LL. It makes them feel more comfortable through cooperative learning, and it reduces their anxiety (Bayat et al., 2017; Buyukkarci, 2010; Tang, 2016; Zhao, 2014). Some publications also mentioned the improvement of their listening skills (Bayat et al., 2017; Caruso et al., 2017; Cummins & Davesne, 2009; Pinto-Llorente et al., 2016).

The use of technologies was mentioned as a factor supporting all of the above (Alam, 2019; Buyukkarci, 2010; Caruso et al., 2017; Karagianni, 2012; Phung, 2016; Tsagari, 2004). This reinforces the student-centred focus of current learning theories and LL approaches which aim to involve students in their language acquisition (Chen & Zhang, 2017; Davison, 2019; Papadima-Sophocleous, 2017). Moreover, two other common findings were the effective provision of feedback and the increase of students' motivation and performances in the target language (Burner, 2016; Chen et al., 2014). It has been highlighted by researchers that FA environments can reduce students' anxiety and make them feel more comfortable using the target language. According to the publications, the focus of the teachers has been on various aspects such as specific assessments and tools used for FA purposes, time considerations in giving feedback, the tendency in some countries for SA practices/preferences, and the lack and need of teacher training in the use of FA in LL. These findings support earlier findings by researchers (Chen et al., 2014; Crusan, Plakans, & Gebril, 2016; Cummins & Davesne, 2009; Kuo, 2015; Vassiliou & Papadima-Sophocleous, 2019; Zhao, 2014). They also indicate the importance of further research in these areas.

The outcomes of the reviewed research also highlighted the lack of teachers' knowledge and training in the application of FA practices, thus reinforcing earlier research on these topics (Crusan et al., 2016; Lam, 2015; Tsagari & Michaeloudes, 2013; Tsagari et al., 2018) and the need for clearer understanding of the relation and or distinction between FA and SA (Leung & Rea-Dickins, 2007).

2.4.7. Languages

Another feature investigated was which languages were represented in research carried out in English in the area of the use of FA in LL (Alam, 2019; Alharbi & Meccawy, 2020; Burner, 2016; Chen & Zhang, 2017; Cotter & Hinkelman, 2019; Joyce, 2018; Levy & Gertler, 2015; Tang, 2016; Vågen, 2017). The results indicated that the dominant language was English as an FL, L2, or EAL, followed by Spanish (Bachelor & Bachelor, 2016; Carreira, 2012; Radford, 2014). One could expect that, in mainly English publications, this is expected. However, in other research written in English and focusing on other aspects related to LL and assessment (testing), languages other than English are more researched. More research is needed in FA in the teaching of other languages beyond English and Spanish. A review of research written in other languages would also enrich our knowledge in the area in further domains as well.

2.4.8. Types of participants

In the 104 publications reviewed in this book, the results indicated a balanced distribution of research in these three different categories of participants: (1)

students (Alam, 2019; Cotter & Hinkelman, 2019; Joyce, 2018; Ranalli, Link, & Chukharev-Hudilainen, 2017), (2) teachers and students (Burner, 2016; Kuo, 2015), and (3) teachers (Guadu & Boersma, 2018; Papadima-Sophocleous, 2017; Wang, 2017). This established that the publications reviewed considered and included all classroom shareholders in their research. As most research recorded was mainly conducted at tertiary education level, future research may bring interesting information to light regarding participants from the other education levels, namely primary and secondary. Future research may also explore other aspects related to FA in LL and participants, such as preferences, similarities, and differences in preferences, etc.

2.4.9. Types of educational levels

It is obvious from the data collected that the dominant educational setting where language FA applications were carried out was that of higher education (Alam, 2019; Guadu & Boersma, 2018; Joyce, 2018; Kızıl & Yumru, 2019; Lam, 2015; Naghdipour, 2017; Papadima-Sophocleous, 2017; Seyyedrezaie et al., 2016; Wang, 2017; Williamson & Sadera, 2016). It is clear that college and university students and teachers had the opportunity to experience more language FA practices than teachers and students in other educational levels, namely primary and secondary. Consequently, it is suggested that more research should be carried out to investigate the reasons for the focus of language FA studies at the tertiary level and to encourage researchers, practitioners, and teachers to include more language FA practices in primary and secondary settings. Findings from tertiary environments could also be made known or shared with primary and secondary educators. Training in FA in LL could also be offered to primary and secondary educators.

2.4.10. Types of FA applications in LL studies

The data revealed that a variety of types of activities and tools such as feedback, portfolio, online quizzes, rubrics, teacher observations, peer-work, tutorials and questioning, discussions, and digital voice recordings were already used in L2 learning for FA purposes (Alam, 2019; Bayat et al., 2017; Carreira, 2012;

Karagianni, 2012; Lam, 2018; Pinto-Llorente et al., 2016). However, since theories of learning, L2 teaching methodologies and technologies constantly develop, more and continuous research is required in the future in under-researched areas and in areas where no research has been carried out so far. A deeper discussion is also needed for the relation of these with the actual nature of FA, as very often they are automatically assumed as FA.

2.4.11. LL focus formatively assessed

To determine the LL focus of the publications under review when analysing the results, the development of this focus and the current trend were identified. Throughout the history of modern language teaching in Europe, the focus of language teaching, learning and assessment depended on the reasons people learned languages and changed through the years (Howatt & Smith, 2014). The findings revealed that the reviewed publications mostly focused on the FA of languages skills and specific aspects such as grammar and vocabulary, based on the traditional language teaching approaches; it did not follow the change of direction which focuses on learning a language to be able to participate in 'real-life' communication, and as a consequence assess formatively 'real-life' communication activities. It is important to also notice that most of this research focused on writing (Alam, 2019; Kızıl & Yumru, 2019; Tavakoli et al., 2018) followed by much less research on speaking (Black & Jones, 2006; Colby-Kelly & Turner, 2007; Cummins & Davesne, 2009; Tuttle & Tuttle, 2013), listening (Bayat et al., 2017; Caruso et al., 2017), reading (Ponce, Mayer, Figueroa, & López, 2018), and other aspects such as vocabulary (Pinto-Llorente et al., 2016; Ponce et al., 2018; Titova, 2015) and grammar (Gan & Leung, 2020; Karagianni, 2012; Titova, 2015).

It would be useful to conduct further research to establish the reason for this preference to writing skills and the reasons why other language skills like reading, speaking, and listening, and other aspects such as grammar and vocabulary have not been yet explored in a great extent. Research should also be carried in the future by researchers to reveal the potentials of FA tools in other aspects and in a more integrative way, reflecting the 'real-life' communication situations which constitute the expected outcome of language education in recent years. 'Real-life' communication FA practices have not yet been investigated to a satisfactory extent. Another interesting finding was that technology was discussed in many publications which dealt with the acquisition of L2 vocabulary and grammar. Further research would also shed light on the use of technologies in FA LL in other aspects such as FA applications for real-life communication.

2.4.12. Learning theories, teaching, and learning approaches and methods in LL FA

The results revealed that only a small number of studies (4.8%) mentioned learning theories, LL, and teaching approaches and methods underpinning the language FA practices they investigated (Chen & Zhang, 2017; Davison, 2019; Kuo, 2015; Little, 2002; Poehner & Lantolf, 2005). This may suggest that specific learning theories, LL, and teaching approaches are implied; it may also suggest that they are not clear to the researchers or they may not feel it is necessary to mention them in their research reports. This lack could be because of other reasons that could be of interest to be identified and discussed. It is suggested that these aspects should be further explored.

2.4.13. Geographic distribution of studies

The study of this aspect unveiled that although research in the practice of FA in LL is carried out globally (in all continents except Antarctica, and in 39 countries), this is not sufficient and extensive compared to the research in SA. However, when it comes to countries, the results indicate that much more research is required globally, in the countries where research already occurs but also in other countries around the world, where such research has not started yet, and establish the reasons why this is not occurring in both cases. It may be either because of their educational systems or because of lack of availability of research funding, it could be because of other reasons that need to be identified and discussed. For example, although the US comes first in research in the area, the percentage of research conducted (22%) is still low; therefore, more research is required in language FA in the US, compared to that conducted for SA. The same goes for all the countries where research in language FA is carried out, as such research is even less than that in the US.

More research should also be carried out to investigate why in countries in Asia, and in specific countries, the rate of interest in language FA practices is higher than in other countries in, for example, Northern America, and Europe. This could be identified by exploring language assessment practices in these countries. According to Chen, Kettle, Klenowski, and May (2013) and Jian and Luo (2014), China's educational system, for example, is based on SA. Added to that, according to Jian and Luo (2014), teachers' level of FA understanding was very low. According to them, this phenomenon could be due to the fact that in China there is low financial support for FA implementations. It could also be because of the relation of the language FA practices to the sociocultural, historical, political, and geographic conditions of China. As stated by Wang (2017), Chinese EFL teachers have difficulty inputting FA theories in action and their assessment practices are dominated by SA with tests and exams. Another explanation may be due to the fact that China belongs to the Confucian Heritage Culture (CHC) with some other Asian countries. In CHC, countries such as China are dominated by examination-oriented environments. According to CHC, a teacher is the authority and plays a key role in the learning process (Chen et al., 2013).

Also, in some studies, it is reported that in traditional educational systems like in China and Japan, interaction is not encouraged and students are sceptical and reluctant to give and accept peer feedback. Silence and listening are more common for them than interacting (Chen et al., 2013). Also, it was found that 90% of Iranian teachers use testing to assess their students as they perceive it as a fairer approach of assessment (Rezaee et al., 2013).

On the other hand, the high number of studies of language FA that took place in China, for example, can explain the quest to change the testing-centred assessment educational system of China. Some research outcomes already support that the inclusion of FA in LL can benefit both students and teachers (Chen et al., 2013; Jian & Luo, 2014; Jiang, 2014; Zhao, 2014). Also, educational systems such as that of Iran connect the alternative type of assessment with a need for more democratic and ethical environments by giving the chance to LL for real-life contextualised practices (Rezaee et al., 2013).

Further and deeper study of the reasons why these countries conduct research in FA in LL may provide useful information which can be shared.

In general, the interest in language FA appears to be gradually taking place globally with a close proportion approximately in all continents. However, more research would be beneficial. Aspects such as the knowledge and practices of FA by the different stakeholders can be further explored, the pros and cons can be discussed, the further development can be further examined, comparison can be made and useful conclusions can be drawn.

2.4.14. Emerged themes

2.4.14.1.Types of technologies in the use of FA in LL

Although the use of technologies in FA in LL did not constitute part of any research question, this emerged as an added theme during the data analysis. This finding complements earlier findings (Cummins & Davesne, 2009; Levy & Gertler, 2015; Pinto-Llorente et al., 2016; Saglam, 2018), which support that technologies can enhance the practice of FA in LL. The findings of this research (15% of language FA types involved technologies) indicate the need for further practices and research in this area.

2.4.14.2.The necessity for training language teachers in language FA practices

Another emerging code was the necessity of in-service and pre-service training for language teachers in LAL with a percentage of 7.5% according to Vogt and Tsagari (2014), who explored the Literacy Assessment (LA) of L2 teachers in seven European countries with 854 participants, as well as the necessity of training L2 Teachers in the use of FA in LL. They have stressed the need to address the current insufficient training in LAL. This has also been confirmed by other researchers. Lam (2015) stated that L2 teachers had little or no training in LA practices. According to Lam (2015), there is a lack of classroom-based assessment practices in Hong Kong. Crusan et al. (2016) have indicated that only 26% of the language teachers who participated had nothing or little training on writing assessment practices and most of them did not assimilate the distinction of FA and SA.

It can be concluded that language teachers could benefit more from FA practices in the future in order to know what and how to effectively assess their students' progress.

2.4.14.3.The necessity for training students in language FA practices

Another emerging theme was that of student training. Some studies reviewed in the research, such as those of Zhao (2010), Restrepo and Nelson (2013), Tsagari and Michaeloudes (2013), Chen et al. (2014), Kuo (2015), Lam (2015), and Crusan et al. (2016) also referred to the importance of training students in FA practices. Also, it was stated that many learners were reluctant to write self-reflections, and teachers admitted that they found it hard to convince them (Chen et al., 2013). Other studies referred to the benefits of such training and the importance of students' awareness and understanding of FA and its practices and benefits in LL. Formative types of assessment enable learners to identify their own strengths and weaknesses and to acquire an awareness of their own skills (Restrepo & Nelson, 2013).

Furthermore, in many exam-oriented countries, it is stated that learners do not feel comfortable or confident in providing peer feedback because of their cultural values or cultural background. Learners are more passive in SA environments and do not accept such positive FA implementations which require critical thinking and self-control (Chen et al., 2013; Jian & Luo, 2014; Jiang, 2014; Liu, 2015; Zhao, 2010).

Therefore, the more proficient and trained the learners are, the more positive and willing they will be in participating in language FA activities that are often used

Part 2

to support FA. According to Herrera and Macías (2015) LAL teacher education should balance both classroom (which also includes formative assessment) and accountability assessments (e.g. large scale standardised tests).

Some suggestions derived from the studies are based on how teachers can support students' training in FA practices. An initial step should start from teachers' clear understanding of FA features (Burner, 2016; Crusan et al., 2016). Then, teachers could guide students on FA practices and let them experience FA through, for example, the use of FA as a means of checklists and self-assessment rubrics, and show them examples of effective feedback before they will apply it in learning. Moreover, follow-up discussions and oral feedback after the provision of feedback with learners will enhance the validity of the provided feedback (Saliu Abdulahi, 2017). All these aspects could be the subject of further research in the use of FA in LL.

2.4.14.4.Other emerged themes

The review of the 104 publications brought to light that beyond the FA of languages skills such as writing, speaking, listening, reading, and aspects such as vocabulary and grammar, research also explored other aspects related to the practice of FA in LL such as the reduction of students' anxiety (Bayat et al., 2017; Ketabi & Ketabi, 2014; Tang, 2016), students' shared understanding of FA, differences related to students' sociocultural conditions, beliefs on teachers' and students' roles, and expectations in the target language (Chen et al., 2013). It would be interesting to see further research conducted in these areas and in other areas still not dealt with in research such as mediation and multilingualism, etc.

2.5. Limitations

A significant limitation of the study was the difficulty in accessing all the papers that were detected. Although a substantial number of papers (16,475) were found, a considerable number (2,816) were not accessible. Their inclusion in this SR would have made a difference in the research findings and given further and more informed and inclusive future directions to the researchers, practitioners, and language teachers. That being said, it would also be safe to say that not all 2,816 would have probably met the criteria of FA as forming the learning of students during the learning process.

Another limitation of the study was the fact that in this SR, only papers written in English were included. One could argue that there is a substantial number of papers published in other languages that have reached important research outcomes related to the use of FA in LL. The present study was considered as a starting point to a more comprehensive study of this area, and a blueprint in terms of the method used.

2.6. Conclusions

The SR, which constitutes Part 2 of this research, can be considered a snapshot of current studies of language FA practices from 2000 to 2020. It has identified, selected, and synthesised primary research studies and provided a picture of the topic being studied (Oakley, 2012). Furthermore, the SR highlighted the impact of FA application in support of language teaching and learning. More specifically, the SR has identified the main trends and issues that are related to language FA: the raise of interest in language FA in recent years; the main research methodologies and research tools that are preferred by the researchers in the area of language FA; the purpose of language FA in the research conducted from 2000 to 2020; the types of research conducted; the main research methodologies and data collection tools that are preferred; the types of outcomes reported in these publications; the languages explored in language FA research; the types of participants; the preferred education levels where language FA was carried out; the types of FA applications practised in LL; the input and the extent of input of technologies; the language focus examined; the locations globally where language FA research was carried out; and the need for training of both students and language teachers in FA. The present SR provides researchers, practitioners, and other interested stakeholders considerable information and background regarding research in the area between 2000 to 2020; it also provides new directions for further research of these issues and supports the role of FA in LL.

The annotated bibliography that follows complements the snapshot provided by the SR, by giving an evaluative description of the main features of each of the 104 reviewed publications.

References

Alam, M. (2019). Assessment challenges & impact of formative portfolio assessment (FPA) on EFL learners' writing performance: a case study on the preparatory English language course. *English Language Teaching, 12*(7), 161-172. https://doi.org/10.5539/elt.v12n7p161

Alharbi, A. S., & Meccawy, Z. (2020). Introducing Socrative as a tool for formative assessment in Saudi EFL classrooms. *Arab World English Journal, 11*(3), 372-384.

Alzaid, F., & Alkarzae, N. (2019). *The effects of paper, web, and gamebased formative assessment on motivation and learning: a literature review.* https://files.eric.ed.gov/fulltext/ED594189.pdf

Ammar, A. (2020). *Impact of formative assessment on raising students' motivation: case of third year EFl students at the university of El-Oued.* Doctoral dissertation. University of Tlemcen.

Bachelor, J. W., & Bachelor, R. B. (2016). Classroom currency as a means of formative feedback, reflection, and assessment in the world language classroom. *NECTFL Review, 78*, 31-42. https://files.eric.ed.gov/fulltext/EJ1256488.pdf

Bahati, B., Tedre, M., Fors, U., & Evode, M. (2016). Exploring feedback practises in formative assessment in Rwandan higher education: a multifaceted approach is needed. *International Journal of Teaching and Education, 4*(2), 1-22. https://doi.org/10.20472/TE.2016.4.2.001

Bayat, A., Jamshidipour, A., & Hashemi, M. (2017). The beneficial impacts of applying formative assessment on Iranian university students' anxiety reduction and listening efficacy. *International Journal of Languages' Education and Teaching, 5*(2), 1-11. https://doi.org/10.18298/ijlet.1740

Black, P., & Jones, J. (2006). Formative assessment and the learning and teaching of MFL: sharing the language learning road map with the learners. *Language Learning Journal, 34*(1), 4-9. https://doi.org/10.1080/09571730685200171

Burner, T. (2014). The potential formative benefits of portfolio assessment in second and foreign language writing contexts: a review of the literature. *Studies in Educational Evaluation, 43*, 139-149. https://doi.org/10.1016/j.stueduc.2014.03.002

Burner, T. (2016). Formative assessment of writing in English as a foreign language. *Scandinavian Journal of Educational Research, 60*(6), 626-648. https://doi.org/10.1080/00313831.2015.1066430

Buyukkarci, K. (2010). *The effect of formative assessment on learners' test anxiety and assessment preferences in EFL context.* Unpublished doctoral dissertation. Cukurova University.

Carreira, M. M. (2012). Formative assessment in HL teaching: purposes, procedures, and practices. *Heritage Language Journal, 9*(1), 100-120. https://doi.org/10.46538/hlj.9.1.6

Caruso, M., Gadd Colombi, A., & Tebbit, S. (2017). Teaching how to listen. Blended learning for the development and assessment of listening skills in a second language. *Journal of University Teaching & Learning Practice, 14*(1), 14. https://files.eric.ed.gov/fulltext/EJ1142367.pdf

Chen, D., & Zhang, L. (2017). Formative assessment of academic English writing for Chinese EFL learners. *TESOL International Journal, 12*(2), 47-64. https://files.eric.ed.gov/fulltext/EJ1247811.pdf

Chen, Q., Kettle, M., Klenowski, V., & May, L. (2013). Interpretations of formative assessment in the teaching of English at two Chinese universities: a sociocultural perspective. *Assessment & Evaluation in Higher Education, 38*(7), 831-846. https://doi.org/10.1080/02602938.2012.726963

Chen, Q., May, L., Klenowski, V., & Kettle, M. (2014). The enactment of formative assessment in English language classrooms in two Chinese universities: teacher and student responses. *Assessment in Education: Principles, Policy & Practice, 21*(3), 271-285. https://doi.org/10.1080/0969594X.2013.790308

Colby-Kelly, C., & Turner, C. E. (2007). AFL research in the L2 classroom and evidence of usefulness: taking formative assessment to the next level. *Canadian Modern Language Review, 64*(1), 9-37. https://doi.org/10.3138/cmlr.64.1.009

Cotter, M., & Hinkelman, D. (2019). Video assessment module: self, peer, and teacher post performance assessment for learning. In F. Meunier, J. Van de Vyver, L. Bradley & S. Thouësny (Eds), *CALL and complexity – short papers from EUROCALL 2019* (pp. 94-99). Research-publishing.net. https://doi.org/10.14705/rpnet.2019.38.992

Creswell, J. W. (2009). *Research design: qualitative, quantitative, and mixed methods approaches* (3rd ed.). Sage Publications.

Crompton H., Burke D., & Gregory, K. H. (2017). The use of mobile learning in PK-12education: a systematic review. *Computers & Education (2017)*. https://doi.org/10.1016/j.compedu.2017.03.013

Crompton, H., Burke, D., & Lin, Y. C. (2019). Mobile learning and student cognition: a systematic review of PK-12 research using Bloom's taxonomy. *British Journal of Educational Technology, 50*(2), 684-701. https://doi.org/10.1111/bjet.12674

Crusan, D., Plakans, L., & Gebril, A. (2016). Writing assessment literacy: surveying second language teachers' knowledge, beliefs, and practices. *Assessing Writing, 28,* 43-56. https://doi.org/10.1016/j.asw.2016.03.001

Cummins, P. W., & Davesne, C. (2009). Using electronic portfolios for second language assessment. *The Modern Language Journal, 93*(1), 848-867. https://doi.org/10.1111/j.1540-4781.2009.00977.x

Davison C. (2019). Using assessment to enhance learning in English language education. In X. Gao (Ed.), *Second handbook of English language teaching. Springer International Handbooks of Education*. Springer. https://doi.org/10.1007/978-3-030-02899-2_21

Elliott, V. (2018). Thinking about the coding process in qualitative data analysis. *The Qualitative Report, 23*(11), 2850-2861. https://doi.org/10.46743/2160-3715/2018.3560

Fakeye, D. O. (2016). Secondary school teachers' and students' attitudes towards formative assessment and corrective feedback in English language in Ibadan Metropolis. *Journal of Educational and Social Research, 6*(2), 141-148. https://doi.org/10.5901/jesr.2016.v6n2p141

Gan, Z., & Leung, C. (2020). Illustrating formative assessment in task-based language teaching. *ELT Journal, 74*(1), 10-19. https://doi.org/10.1093/ELT/CCZ048

Graham, S., Harris, K. R., & Hebert, M. A. (2011). *Informing writing: the benefits of formative assessment. A Carnegie Corporation Time to Act Report.* Alliance for Excellence in Education. https://www.carnegie.org/publications/informing-writing-the-benefits-of-formative-assessment/

Guadu, Z. B., & Boersma, E. J. (2018). EFL instructors' beliefs and practices of formative assessment in teaching writing. *Journal of Language Teaching and Research, 9*(1), 42-50. https://doi.org/10.17507/jltr.0901.06

Haines, K., Meima, E., & Faber, M. (2013). Formative assessment and the support of lecturers in the international university. In *International experiences in language testing and assessment* (pp. 177-190). Peter Lang.

Hansson, S. (2015). *Benefits and difficulties in using peer response for writing in the EFL classroom.* Göteborgs Universitet. https://gupea.ub.gu.se/bitstream/2077/38436/1/gupea_2077_38436_1.pdf

Herrera L., & Macías, D. F. (2015). A call for language assessment literacy in the education and development of teachers of English as a foreign language. *Colombian Applied Linguistics Journal, 17*(2), 302-312. https://doi.org/10.14483/udistrital.jour.calj.2015.2.a09

Howatt, A. P. R., & Smith, R. (2014). The history of teaching English as a foreign language, from a British and European perspective. *Language & History, 57*(1), 75-95. https://doi.org/10.1179/1759753614Z.00000000028

Huang, S. C. (2016). No longer a teacher monologue – involving EFL writing learners in teachers' assessment and feedback processes. *Taiwan Journal of TESOL, 13*(1), 1-31. http://www.tjtesol.org/attachments/article/402/04_TJTESOL-273.pdf

Jian, H., & Luo, S. (2014). Formative assessment in L2 classroom in China: the current situation, predicament and future. *Indonesian Journal of Applied Linguistics, 3*(2), 18-34. https://doi.org/10.17509/ijal.v3i2.266

Jiang, Y. (2014). Exploring teacher questioning as a formative assessment strategy. *RELC Journal, 45*(3), 287-304. https://doi.org/10.1177/0033688214546962

Joyce, P. (2018). The effectiveness of online and paper-based formative assessment in the Learning of English as a second language. *PASAA, 5,* 126-146. https://www.culi.chula.ac.th/publicationsonline/files/article/W8Mo0m4nyBMon110741.pdf

Karagianni, E. (2012). Employing computer assisted assessment (CAA) to facilitate formative assessment in the State Secondary School: a case study. *Research Papers in Language Teaching and Learning, 3*(1), 252-268.

Ketabi, S., & Ketabi, S. (2014). Classroom and formative assessment in second/foreign language teaching and learning. *Theory & Practice in Language Studies, 4*(2), 435-440. https://doi.org/10.4304/tpls.4.2.435-440

Kızıl, V., & Yumru, H. (2019). The impact of self-assessment: a case study on a tertiary level EFL writing class. *Mevzu – Sosyal Bilimler Dergisi, 1,* 35-54.

Kuo, C. L. (2015). *A quasi-experimental study of formative peer assessment in an EFL writing classroom.* Unpublished doctoral dissertation. Newcastle University. http://theses.ncl.ac.uk/jspui/handle/10443/2863

Lam, R. (2015). Language assessment training in Hong Kong: implications for language assessment literacy. *Language Testing, 32*(2), 169-197. https://doi.org/10.1177/0265532214554321

Lam, R. (2018). Understanding assessment as learning in writing classrooms: the case of portfolio assessment. *Iranian Journal of Language Teaching Research, 6*(3), 19-36. https://doi.org/10.30466/ijltr.2018.120599

Leung, C., & Rea-Dickins, P. (2007). Teacher assessment as policy instrument: contradictions and capacities. *Language Assessment Quarterly, 4*(1), 6-36. https://doi.org/10.1080/15434300701348318

Levy, T., & Gertler, H. (2015). Harnessing technology to assess oral communication in Business English. *Teaching English with Technology, 15*(4), 52-59. https://files.eric.ed.gov/fulltext/EJ1138436.pdf

Little, D. (2002). The European Language Portfolio: structure, origins, implementation and challenges. *Language Teaching, 35*(3), 182-189. https://doi.org/10.1017/S0261444802001805

Liu, X. (2015). The application of formative assessment in College English Teaching. *Proceedings of the 1st International Conference on Arts, Design and Contemporary Education* (pp. 875-879). ICADCE, 2015. https://doi.org/10.2991/icadce-15.2015.211

McKim, C. A. (2017). The value of mixed methods research: a mixed methods study. *Journal of Mixed Methods Research, 11*(2), 202-222. https://doi.org/10.1177/1558689815607096

Medelyan, A. (2020). *Coding qualitative data: how to code qualitative research.* InSights. https://getthematic.com/insights/coding-qualitative-data/

Meissner, M. C. (2018). *Formative assessment at the intersection of principles, practice and perceptions.* Master's thesis. Faculty of Education and Natural Sciences, Inland Norway University of Applied Sciences.

Meline, T. (2006). Selecting studies for systematic review: inclusion and exclusion criteria. *Contemporary issues in Communication Science and Disorders, 33,* 21-27. https://doi.org/10.1044/cicsd_33_S_21

Memorial University Libraries. (n.d.). *How to evaluate information resources.* https://www.library.mun.ca/researchtools/guides/doingresearch/evaluateall/

Naghdipour, B. (2017). Incorporating formative assessment in Iranian EFL writing: a case study. *The Curriculum Journal, 28*(2), 283-299. https://doi.org/10.1080/09585176.2016.1206479

Oakley, A. (2012). Foreword. In D. Gough, S. Oliver & J. Thomas (Eds), *An introduction to systematic reviews* (pp. vii-x). Sage Publications.

Papadima-Sophocleous, S. (2017). L2 assessment and testing teacher education: an exploration of alternative assessment approaches using new technologies. In K. Borthwick, L. Bradley & S. Thouësny (Eds), *CALL in a climate of change: adapting to turbulent global conditions – short papers from EUROCALL 2017* (pp. 248-253). Research-publishing.net. https://doi.org/10.14705/rpnet.2017.eurocall2017.721

Phung, H. V. (2016). Portfolio assessment in second/foreign language pedagogy. *Hawaii Pacific University TESOL Working Paper Series 14*, 90-107. https://www.hpu.edu/research-publications/tesol-working-papers/2016/07HuyPhung.pdf

Pinto-Llorente, A. M., Sánchez-Gómez, M. C., García-Peñalvo, F. J., & Martín, S. C. (2016, November). The use of online quizzes for continuous assessment and self-assessment of second-language learners. In *Proceedings of the Fourth International Conference on Technological Ecosystems for Enhancing Multiculturality* (pp. 819-824). https://doi.org/10.1145/3012430.3012612

Piper, R. J. (2013). How to write a systematic literature review: a guide for medical students. *NSAMR*. University of Edinburg. https://sites.cardiff.ac.uk/curesmed/files/2014/10/NSAMR-Systematic-Review.pdf

Poehner, M. E., & Lantolf, J. P. (2005). Dynamic assessment in the language classroom. *Language Teaching Research, 9*(3), 233-265. https://doi.org/10.1191/1362168805lr166oa

Ponce, H. R., Mayer, R. E., Figueroa, V. A., & López, M. J. (2018). Interactive highlighting for just-in-time formative assessment during whole-class instruction: effects on vocabulary learning and reading comprehension. *Interactive Learning Environments, 26*(1), 42-60. https://doi.org/10.1080/10494820.2017.1282878

Poole, F. J., & Clarke-Midura, J. (2020). A systematic review of digital games in second language learning studies. *International Journal of Game-Based Learning (IJGBL), 10*(3), 1-15. https://doi.org/10.4018/IJGBL.2020070101

Qualitative Variables. (2009). In *Nelson Mathematics Secondary Year Two, Cycle One* (pp.1-4). Nelson Education. http://www.nelson.com/school/elementary/mathK8/quebec/0176237879/documents/NM8SB_3A.pdf?fbclid=IwAR3DNvF45J8yvf-oyvyHPNSd-Eg3M1s1aPAlLu7LvE77tL91hySintkarto

Radford, B. W. (2014). *The effect of formative assessments on languageperformance*. Unpublished doctoral dissertation. Brigham Young, Provo. http://scholarsarchive.byu.edu/etd/3978

Ranalli, J., Link, S., & Chukharev-Hudilainen, E. (2017). Automated writing evaluation for formative assessment of second language writing: investigating the accuracy and usefulness of feedback as part of argument-based validation. *Educational Psychology, 37*(1), 8-25. https://doi.org/10.1080/01443410.2015.1136407

Rea-Dickins, P. (2004). Understanding teachers as agents of assessment. *Language Testing, 21*(3), 249-258. https://doi.org/10.1191/0265532204lt283ed

Rea-Dickins, P., & Gardner, S. (2000). Snares and silver bullets: disentangling the construct of formative assessment. *Language Testing, 17*(2), 215-243. https://doi.org/10.1177/026553220001700206

Restrepo, A., & Nelson, H. (2013). Role of systematic formative assessment on students' views of their learning. *Profile Issues in Teachers Professional Development, 15*(2), 165-183. http://www.scielo.org.co/scielo.php?pid=S1657-07902013000200011&script=sci_arttext&tlng=pt

Rezaee, A. A., Alavi, S. M., & Shabani, E. A. (2013). Alternative assessment or traditional testing: how do Iranian EFL teachers respond? *Teaching English Language, 7*(2), 151-190.

Saglam, A. L. G. (2018). The integration of educational technology for classroom-based formative assessment to empower teaching and learning. In A. Khan & S. Umair (Eds), *Handbook of research on mobile devices and smart gadgets in K-12 rducation* (pp. 321-341). IGI Global. https://doi.org/10.4018/978-1-5225-2706-0.ch020

Saldaña, J. (2015). *The coding manual for qualitative researchers*. Sage.

Saliu Abdulahi, D. (2017). Scaffolding writing development: how formative is the feedback? *Moderna språk, 111*(1), 127-155. https://www.duo.uio.no/handle/10852/59613

Saoud, A. (2016). *Impact of formative assessment on raising students' motivation: case of third year EFL students at the University of El-Oued*. Unpublished doctoral dissertation. University of Tlemcen.

Seyyedrezaie, Z. S., Ghansoli, B., Shahriari, H., & Fatemi, A. H. (2016). Examining the effects of Google docs-based instruction and peer feedback types (implicit vs. explicit) on EFL learners' writing performance. *CALL-EJ, 17*(1), 35-51. http://callej.org/journal/17-1/Seyyedrezaie_Ghonsooly_Shahriari_Fatemi2016.pdf

Smith, D. H., & Davis, J. E. (2014). Formative assessment for student progress and programme improvement in sign language as L2 programmes. In D. McKee, R. S. Rosen & R. McKee (Eds), *Teaching and learning signed languages* (pp. 253-280). Palgrave Macmillan. https://doi.org/10.1057/9781137312495_12

Spolaôr, N., & Benitti, F. B. V. (2017). Robotics applications grounded in learning theories on tertiary education: a systematic review. *Computers & Education, 112*, 97-107. https://doi.org/10.1016/j.compedu.2017.05.001

Tang, L. (2016). Formative assessment in oral English classroom and alleviation of speaking apprehension. *Theory and Practice in Language Studies, 6*(4), 751-756. https://doi.org/10.17507/tpls.0604.12

Tavakoli, E., Amirian, S. M. R., Burner, T., Davoudi, M., & Ghaniabadi, S. (2018). Operationalization of formative assessment in writing: an intuitive approach to the development of an instrument. *Applied Research on English Language, 7*(3), 319-344. https://doi.org/10.22108/ARE.2018.112373.1340

The University of Melbourne. (2021). *Common inclusion/exclusion criteria*. https://unimelb.libguides.com/c.php?g=492361&p=3368110

Titova, S. (2015). Use of mobile testing system PeLe for developing language skills. In F. Helm, L. Bradley, M. Guarda & S. Thouësny (Eds), *Critical CALL – proceedings of the 2015 EUROCALL Conference* (pp. 523-528). Research-publishing.net. https://doi.org/10.14705/rpnet.2015.000387

Tsagari, D. (2004). Is there life beyond language testing? An introduction to alternative language assessment. *CRILE Working Papers, 58*, 1-23. https://pdfs.semanticscholar.org/19ad/ddb4879992814f8ebbc323a8d6f2dd491a4f.pdf

Tsagari, D. (2016). Assessment orientations of state primary EFL teachers in two Mediterranean countries. *Center for Educational Policy Studies Journal, 6*(1), 9-30. https://doi.org/10.26529/cepsj.102

Tsagari, D., & Michaeloudes, G. (2013). Formative assessment patterns in CLIL primary schools in Cyprus. In S. Ioannou-Georgiou, S. Papadima-Sophocleous & D. Tsagari (Eds), *International experiences in language testing and assessment* (pp. 75-93). Peter Lang Edition.

Tsagari, D., Vogt, K., Froelich, V., Csépes, I., Fekete, A., Green A., Hamp-Lyons, L., Sifakis, N., & Kordia, S. (2018). *Handbook of assessment for language teachers*. https://taleproject.eu/pluginfile.php/2129/mod_page/content/12/TALE%20Handbook%20-%20colour.pdf

Tuttle, H. G., & Tuttle, A. (2013). *Improving foreign language speaking through formative assessment*. Routledge. https://doi.org/10.4324/9781315854854

Vågen, M. T. (2017). *Formative assessment in EFL writing: a case study of pupils' perceptions of their feedback practice and attitudes to receiving and using feedback*. Master's thesis. University of Bergen.

Vassiliou, S., & Papadima-Sophocleous, S. (2019). A systematic review and annotated bibliography of second language learning formative assessment: an overview. *Conference Proceedings, 12th International Conference Innovation in Language Learning* (pp. 352-362). https://conference.pixel-online.net/ICT4LL/files/ict4ll/ed0012/Conference%20Proceedings.pdf

Vogt, K., & Tsagari, D. (2014). Assessment literacy of foreign language teachers: findings of a European study. *Language Assessment Quarterly, 11*(4), 374-402. https://doi.org/10.1080/15434303.2014.960046

Wang, X. (2017). A Chinese EFL teacher's classroom assessment practices. *Language Assessment Quarterly, 14*(4), 312-327. https://doi.org/10.1080/15434303.2017.1393819

Widiastuti, I. A. M. S., Mukminatien, N., Prayogo, J. A., & Irawati, E. (2020). Dissonances between teachers' beliefs and practices of formative assessment in EFL classes. *International Journal of Instruction, 13*(1), 71-84. https://doi.org/10.29333/iji.2020.1315a

Widiastuti, I. A. M. S., & Saukah, A. (2017). Formative assessment in EFL classroom practices. *Bahasa dan Seni: Jurnal Bahasa, Sastra, Seni, dan Pengajarannya, 45*(1), 50-63. https://doi.org/10.17977/um015v45i12017p050

Williamson, K., & Sadera, E. (2016). Electronic formative feedback and its effect on the writing skills of Asian L2 postgraduate students. *DEANZ2016: Conference Proceedings* (pp. 208-210). https://kiwibelma.files.wordpress.com/2016/05/deanz16-conference-proceedings11-april.pdf

Wolf, M. K., Shore, J. R., & Blood, I. (2014). *English learner formative assessment (ELFA): a design framework.* ETS.

Yarahmadzehi, N., & Goodarzi, M. (2020). Investigating the role of formative mobile based assessment in vocabulary learning of pre-intermediate EFL learners in comparison with paper based assessment. *Turkish Online Journal of Distance Education, 21*(1), 181-196.

Zhao, H. (2010). Investigating learners' use and understanding of peer and teacher feedback on writing: a comparative study in a Chinese English writing classroom. *Assessing writing, 15*(1), 3-17. https://doi.org/10.1016/j.asw.2010.01.002

Zhao, H. (2014). Investigating teacher-supported peer assessment for EFL writing. *ELT Journal, 68*(2), 155-168. https://doi.org/10.1093/elt/cct068

Formative assessments are the way a classroom teacher can check to make sure everyone arrives at the destination of learning.

Jennifer Beasley

PART 3

An annotated bibliography in formative assessment in language learning

3.1. Introduction

As previously mentioned, this book tells the story of Formative Assessment (FA) in LL in two ways: the first, in Part II, is in the form of a Systematic Review (SR) and the second, in Part III, in the form of a descriptive and evaluative Annotated Bibliography (AB), the one complementing the other.

In Part II, the SR identified, selected, and synthesised primary research studies (Oakley, 2012), provided an overview of FA in Language Learning (LL) in a chronological order, from the very first published work on the subject in 2000 to 2020, and highlighted the impact of FA application in LL, during the designated period.

In Part III, the AB, on the other hand, gives more details for each research work. It focuses on the importance of each source (Buttram, MacMillan, & Koch, 2012) in relation to the topic. It pays particular attention to the content and contribution of each individual source to the given area of research. Each entry can be defined as a brief explanatory or evaluative note of each reference or citation (Buttram et al., 2012). An annotation can be helpful to the researcher in informing him about the source and evaluating whether the source is relevant to a given topic or line of inquiry.

An investigation in the area of FA in LL research has revealed that there is no AB in the use of FA in LL. Therefore, the aims of this third part of the book are to fill this gap and to complement the findings of the SR presented earlier in this book.

3.2. Methodology

This descriptive and evaluative AB is organised in chronological order to illustrate the progress in FA LL research (Engle, 2017; Harner, 2000). It provides a more detailed overview of available research sources on the specific topic of FA in LL. It consists of a series of bibliographical entries and citations, each one describing a different source (Harner, 2000). It follows the same research design and the same methods used in the SR section to identify, include, and/or exclude possible sources.

The total number of annotations is 104 based on the inclusion/exclusion criteria employed. The AB consists of a series of annotations of about 300 words each. Each annotation first includes a citation in APA style 7th edition. The citation is followed by a description of the content of each publication with evaluative comments. Entries of annotations include articles, books, chapters, conference proceedings papers, reports, short papers, and PhD theses published in the English language from 2000-2020. However, instead of synthesising different studies related to language FA practices, it focuses on the description and evaluation of each publication. The AB presents by annotation the research that has been conducted each year, within the specific period of 20 years (2000-2020). Each source is described in a summative paragraph which evaluatively describes the content of the source (Harner, 2000). The evaluative description of each source gives a clear idea of how, when and under what circumstances teachers or researchers conducted research in the area of FA, and how their studies perceived FA.

The descriptive part refers to information such as the type of the publication, the country where the study was conducted, or, in some cases, the type of research that was followed by the researcher, a short statement that explains the main focus or purposes of the work, a short description of the work, a short summary of the theory of learning that frames the FA (if mentioned), characteristics and practices of FA, research findings, intended audience, subject(s) covered, major arguments supported, data collection tools, conclusions reached, and special features.

Additionally, the evaluative part includes a consideration of the usefulness and/or limitations of the text for L2 FA research by exploring aspects such as quality of the evidence, the publication's place in the academic conversation, poor features, weaknesses in argument, and the value of the source to the L2 FA research (Buttram et al., 2012; Harner, 2000).

The following criteria, based on different sources (Memorial University Libraries, n.d.; UNSW Sydney Current Students, n.d.; The Writing Center, University of Colorado Denver | Anschutz Medical Campus, 2014), were used in order to conduct this AB:

- complete bibliographic citation;

- publication date, within the period studied: 2000-2020;

- type of publications: journal articles, conference proceedings papers, short papers, book chapters, books, handbooks, Doctoral or Master theses, reports;

- publisher: e.g. university press, reputable publisher;

- authors' credibility and reliability: institutional affiliation, educational background, past writing experience as it relates to research, text written in the author's area of expertise, the author has been mentioned in lectures or cited in other sources or bibliographies;

- scope and main purpose of the work: main arguments;

- research methods: QUAL; QUAN; mixed);

- reliability of the text;

- content and objective reasoning: based on fact, not opinion or propaganda, information is valid and well-researched, not questionable and unsupported by evidence, with reasonable assumptions and no errors or omissions. Ideas and arguments are advanced more or less in line with other works on the same topic and the author's point of view is objective and impartial, with a language free of bias;

- content coverage: the work updates other sources, substantiates other materials, or adds new information. It extensively or marginally covers the research topic. Enough sources are read to obtain a variety of viewpoints and the material is primary (raw material of the research process such as journal articles presenting new findings, diaries, speeches, manuscripts, letters, interviews, new film footage, autobiographies, or official records) or secondary (based on primary sources such as textbooks, magazine articles, histories, criticisms, commentaries, or encyclopaedias) source in nature. It is best to use a mixture of primary and secondary sources if possible;

- relevancy: the publication fully or only partially covers the topic: the reference made to FA is actually forming learning, it is assessment for learning not just claiming to be;

- text strengths and limitations;

- accuracy/validity: are the conclusions reached by the author supported by the evidence used: is it FA or is it just a claim? Is there a use of an e-portfolio for FA or is it just a claim? Is only one side of a topic discussed? Are there any typographical errors (spelling mistakes, poor grammar, etc.)? Were external sources consulted and properly cited?

- intended audience: is the work intended for scholars, professionals, or the general public? Is the level of content appropriate or is it too detailed/specialised, or too general/simple;

- writing style and correctness;

- in what way the text relates to themes or concepts in our book; and

- how the source compares to other books, articles, etc. on the same topic.

Publications that met at least 70% of the evaluative criteria were included in this AB.

The aim of this critical evaluative AB is to complement the findings and outcomes of the SR of the research publications discussed in this book, by providing more information on each publication, in the form of a description and evaluation of the main features. It is hoped that it will fill the gap in FA in LL scholarly research, and it will be a solid basis for further research by teachers or educators who would like to investigate the affordances of language FA.

3.3. Annotated bibliography entries

Rea-Dickins, P., & Gardner, S. (2000). Snares and silver bullets: disentangling the construct of formative assessment. *Language Testing, 17*(2), 215-243. https://doi.org/10.1177/026553220001700206

> This peer-reviewed article presents an investigation from the UK concentrating on FA implementations in nine inner-city schools. Based on the Early Years Intervention Project, this research deals with English language learners (Key Stage 1, five to seven years old) who studied English as an Additional Language with low levels of achievement. Using a case study, the authors, authorities in assessment, interviewed EAL teachers and observed their classes and found that decisions made during lessons for students' performance were important. According to the authors, results revealed that implementations of FA raise many issues. One of the biggest issues that is mentioned is the skills that teachers should have to conduct FA, especially in observing students in real time lessons. Also, collaboration between staff with ESL students is important in implementing discussions, planning, and assessments. The

authors stressed the importance of clear distinction between formative and summative assessment. The issue of reliability of types of FA like observations was also mentioned. These are highly important issues to take into consideration before implementing FA. This is considered as the first publication that is focused on FA in LL and it has been cited many times in other sources or bibliographies. It has an important value in FA LL research.

Gattullo, F. (2000). Formative assessment in ELT primary (elementary) classrooms: an Italian case study. *Language Testing, 17*(2), 278-288. https://doi.org/10.1177/026553220001700210

This peer-reviewed article presents a pilot case study that was carried out in two primary schools in Northern Italy over a period of two years (1997-1998). Four teachers, three specialists, one generalist and 86 pupils (aged from nine to ten years old) who studied EFL participated in this study. Lesson observations, teachers' interviews, questionnaires to students, and an analysis of assessment tools were used to collect data about FA implementations. Findings have shed some light in specific areas: for example, oral assessment should be more structured; the use of feedback enables students to improve themselves. The value of this case study is that it is one of the first studies which paid attention to FA and EFL teaching and learning. The author is affiliated with a reputable university in Italy. The author's research work has been extensively cited in other sources.

Little, D. (2002). The European Language Portfolio: structure, origins, implementation and challenges. *Language Teaching, 35*(3), 182-189. https://doi.org/10.1017/S0261444802001805

The author of this peer-reviewed article was Director of the Centre for Language and Communication Studies and Associate Professor of Applied Linguistics at Trinity College, Dublin, Co-ordinator of the Council of Europe's European Language Portfolio project, and a consultant to the European Validation Committee, which was responsible for accrediting European Language Portfolio models, at the time. In this article, he describes the structure, origins, implementation, and challenges of the ELP, and the measures taken to encourage large-scale implementation of ELP. As he has widely published on the theory and practice of learner autonomy in second and foreign LL, he also discusses the pedagogical challenge of the ELP: focusing on learner self-assessment, he acknowledges the teachers' concerns for the students' abilities to assess themselves. However, he refers to three ELP elements that respond to these worries: the 'can do' statements, the comparison of learners' self-assessment with other types of assessment such as examination grades and work collected in their dossier, and the focus of ELP, be it FA or SA. He supports that, while ELP passport self-assessment is more of an SA nature, the use of ELP language biography, where learners set learning goals or monitor progress, is more of an FA nature. Little also referred to learners' autonomy (responsibility for their own learning, and exercise this responsibility in a continuous effort to understand their learning process) and the importance of reflection. The ELP has influenced LL and assessment. Little's article contributes to the understanding of ELP and its implementation.

Carless, D. R. (2002). The mini-viva as a tool to enhance assessment for learning. *Assessment & Evaluation in Higher Education, 27*(4), 353-363. https://doi.org/10.1080/0260293022000001364

This peer-reviewed article presents an action-research conducted at Hong Kong Institute of Education (HKI) that illustrates the important role of lecturers' feedback provided to students. Following from Boud, Cohen, and Sampson (1999) and Black and Wiliam (1998), it aimed to "place particular emphasis on assessment for learning or the formative aspects of assessment" (Carless, 2002, p. 354). It maintains that FA tools (feedback, student's self-evaluative work, peer collaboration, and feedback) must be used in order to achieve better learning outcomes. This action research was carried out at HKI (the main provider of teacher education in Hong Kong) with 50 future English teachers. The main focus was on a 'mini viva', which was mainly a post-submission tutorial, lasting 15-20 minutes, in which a group of students answered queries about their completed assignments and received feedback. The students' performances in the mini viva were not assessed. Data included oral and written evaluation data from students, two peer observers, and instructors taking part in the action research team. Results showed that student feedback was positive about the process of doing their assignment, although they would have preferred the assignment description be more explicit. The author also mentioned some limitations: the mini-viva may not be feasible with one lecturer only; it may be more feasible with small groups of students; it presupposes students' agreement to participate in an innovative assessment method; a mini-viva may be more suitable to a module on assessment rather than any other type of module. Practicality in terms of workload was also mentioned as a possible limitation. Overall, the author argued that the mini-viva could be a useful tool in one's repertoire of techniques in FA. The author concluded by posing some wider questions for further reflection on FA practises. This publication is useful for two reasons: first it adds mini-viva as a form of FA in the topics of this AB, in other words it adds to the range of FA types of implementations, and second, it could be a starting point for further study.

Rea-Dickins, P. (2004). Understanding teachers as agents of assessment. *Language Testing, 21*(3), 249-258. https://doi.org/10.1191/0265532204lt283ed

This *Language Testing* journal editorial (UK), by Rea-Dickins, discusses the role of the classroom teacher as an agent of assessment. In a climate where the emphasis was given to summative measures of learner performance, both in assessment practices and in assessment research, Rea-Dickins introduced the importance of classroom teacher assessment and its further understanding, depicted in the articles of this volume. After noting the relatively under-researched issue, the author emphasised the need for research in teacher assessment or classroom-based assessment. She first describes the research already conducted in the relationships between assessment and instruction: impact of assessment – formal examinations and assessment frameworks – on classroom instruction; the role of the teacher and the "links between assessment and instruction in terms of the authenticity and congruence of assessment practises in relation to a particular programme of study" (p. 250); and the success of a language programme in terms of learner attainment. Part of the review of research conducted was that of the construct of classroom FA, and the difference in the definition of agent (teacher) and purpose (formative/summative) of assessment. The author then describes the articles of the volume, which revolve around the following topics: teacher's 'diagnostic competence'; how teachers arrive at their grading decisions; teachers' beliefs about and their reported understandings of assessment within different national contexts; the role of standards and criteria in teacher assessment processes; current conceptualisations of formative teacher assessment that has the potential to drive LL forward; current conceptualisations of classroom-based assessment from general educational assessment perspectives; and a comparative survey of teacher assessment practices in three different tertiary institutional contexts, Canada, Hong Kong, and China.

Tsagari, D. (2004). Is there life beyond language testing? An introduction to alternative language assessment. *CRILE Working Papers, 58,* 1-23. https://pdfs.semanticscholar.org/19ad/ddb4879992814f8ebbc323a8d6f2dd491a4f.pdf

This peer-reviewed paper published in the UK is an introduction to FA. Its aim is to familiarise readers with what FA entails. It also opens a discussion on some related issues. It presents the main concepts of alternative assessment in language testing and assessment. Tsagari (2004) points out that test-driven environments produce anxiety and stress to students, they do not reflect the students' progress and they overemphasise the grading system. Moreover, the author provides more definitions of assessment that are related to alternative assessment like authentic assessment, continuous assessment, and ongoing assessment. In addition, she gives examples of positive impacts of alternative assessment implementations. Further to presenting its positive aspects, the author also presents some concerns about alternative assessment: providing feedback is considered as time consuming for teachers especially when they have a big number of students. In general, this paper can be considered as a useful guideline to alternative assessment in L2/FL assessment. As the author argues, alternative types of assessment can be more useful and informative compared to test scores. It is also supported that descriptive information and the ongoing measurement of students' progress are important for formative evaluation. This information cannot be collected by tests and scores. Therefore, in this article, FA is presented as an important type of alternative assessment in language teaching and learning.

Poehner, M. E., & Lantolf, J. P. (2005). Dynamic assessment in the language classroom. *Language Teaching Research*, *9*(3), 233-265. https://doi.org/10.1191/1362168805lr166oa

The authors of this paper focus on dynamic assessment in L2. They first discuss Vygotsky's theory of ZPD, on which DA is based, and Reuven Feuerstein's work on DA. The authors then compare DA to FA and suggest ways FA can capitalise on DA. They provide examples from an L2 DA project. They criticise the view that FA procedures are less systematic compared to those of SA, and suggest that FA can be performed systematically. They give examples of how it can be reframed based on DA. This chapter adds to the discussion of FA as it discusses the relationship between FA and DA.

Black, P., & Jones, J. (2006). Formative assessment and the learning and teaching of MFL: sharing the language learning road map with the learners. *Language Learning Journal*, *34*(1), 4-9. https://doi.org/10.1080/09571730685200171

This peer-reviewed article from the UK discusses the integration of FA in LL. It presents descriptions of FA applications emphasising on providing feedback in speaking and writing skills and on peer and self-assessment. It is worth mentioning that the authors offer suggestions to teachers for FA implementations in order to improve their teaching and students' learning outcomes. Also, the main elements of FA practice are presented and at the end some guidance to teachers is provided on how to develop FA practices. This article contributes to a better understanding of FA and its implementation by teachers.

Colby-Kelly, C., & Turner, C. E. (2007). AFL research in the L2 classroom and evidence of usefulness: taking formative assessment to the next level. *Canadian Modern Language Review, 64*(1), 9-37. https://doi.org/10.3138/cmlr.64.1.009

This peer-reviewed article moves on beyond seeking FA as AFL and explores the usefulness of FA and AFL. It investigates the importance of FA in the L2 classroom in a Canadian context. A mixed-method approach was used. This included questionnaires, interviews, classroom observations, and curriculum documents. The data were collected from pre-university EAP classes. The participants consisted of nine teachers and 42 students. Five types of feedback for speaking tasks are described in this article. Findings revealed that teachers and students were positive in supporting FA implementations. It is worth mentioning that authors suggest that language teachers should consider the importance of FA in their teaching. This article adds to the discussion not only of FA as a form of language classroom assessment in general but of FA in an EAP classroom.

Leung, C., & Rea-Dickins, P. (2007). Teacher assessment as policy instrument: contradictions and capacities. *Language Assessment Quarterly, 4*(1), 6-36. https://doi.org/10.1080/15434300701348318

The main argument of this peer-reviewed article is that the official educational assessment policy in England and Wales is not concerned with issues related to different forms of assessment, such as technical, pedagogic and epistemological. In the first part of the article, and with the assessment of English within the national curriculum in mind, the authors discuss the use of assessment as an educational policy instrument and some of the consequences for pedagogy and curriculum provision. In the second part, the main argument is further explored and supported by data collected in relation to the assessment of EAL for students whose L1 language is a language other than English. The authors mention that standardised tests in the UK were preferred to teacher assessment and were seen as more trustworthy measures of assessment. However, low-scores of standardised testing suggest that teacher assessment and FA can gain more interest and attention from teachers and researchers. This article also discusses the official guidance for teacher assessment for EAL students in the UK. The authors state that more teachers see themselves as test developers or examiners. Finally, Leung and Rea-Dickins suggest that a clearer distinction between summative assessment and FA should be promoted to teachers, and a better knowledge of assessment for English as a native language and EAL should be acquired. All the arguments and the examples stress the need for more critical analysis of both policy and practice for the benefit of more equitable and educationally valid assessment. Many readers would identify that the issues discussed here are of concern in many similar contexts. The information shared in this article, therefore, may prove useful to them, particularly the need for clearer understanding of summative assessment and FA.

Cummins, P. W., & Davesne, C. (2009). Using electronic portfolios for second language assessment. *The Modern Language Journal, 93*(1), 848-867. https://doi.org/10.1111/j.1540-4781.2009.00977.x

This peer-reviewed article describes e-portfolio models used in Europe and the United States: the ELP, LF, and GLP. It also reviews assessment scales of e-portfolios (CEFR and ACTFL). The authors also mention the significant benefits of using an e-portfolio rather than a paper and pencil-based portfolio; some of them are interactivity, wide storage of media files, cooperative learning, and artefacts. It then explores the effectiveness of e-portfolios and language assessment and discusses future directions that should be followed. The FA aspects of portfolios are discussed: portfolio construction can be an assessment activity designed to help students learn, be given feedback by the instructor, and have the opportunity to discuss their work with their instructor. The language biography component of a portfolio gives the opportunity for formative self-assessment. The language passport, audio files, and videos illustrate development in speaking and listening but also illustrate gestures, reactions and behaviours. The source highlights the importance of implementing a technology-enhanced environment in portfolio PA for L2 assessment purposes. This article adds to the research already conducted in the use of e-portfolios for LL FA purposes.

Buyukkarci, K. (2010). *The effect of formative assessment on learners' test anxiety and assessment preferences in EFL context.* Unpublished doctoral dissertation. Cukurova University. http://libratez.cu.edu.tr/tezler/8059.pdf

This PhD dissertation from Turkey presents a pilot study. This study investigates the effects of FA on test anxiety and the possibility FA influences students' assessment preferences. A mixed-method was implemented for data collection. The Test Anxiety Inventory was used as a collection of triangulation data to show how students felt about tests in their lives, and what kind of effects those tests had on them through an assessment preference scale, semi-structured interviews, and teachers' observations. Participants were students from Cukurova University English Language Teaching Department. They were divided into a control (38) and an experimental group (48). Results revealed that after post-tests total means show statistically significant difference between the experimental and the control group. The experimental group's mean reveals that there is a decrease after FA implementation while the control group's post-test mean remains the same as at the beginning of the study. Moreover, the results on students' preferences regarding feedback showed that they liked both written and verbal feedback. Also, it is stated that peer assessment enabled learners to reduce their anxiety and felt more confident and willing to work in class. According to the author, one of the reasons this research was conducted was that FA is not considered as an integral part of language teaching in Turkey. Instead, there is a focus on SA preferences. His PhD dissertation contributes to the awareness of FA implementation in places such as Turkey, where FA does not yet constitute an important part of LL.

Absalom, M., & De Saint Léger, D. (2011). Reflecting on reflection learner perceptions of diaries and blogs in tertiary language study. *Arts and Humanities in Higher Education, 10*(2), 189-211. https://doi.org/10.1177/1474022210389141

This peer-reviewed article presents an Australian case study that compares two different types of reflective tasks; an online blog and a traditional pen-and-paper journal. This comparison was conducted in two language courses, one in French (blog) and one in Italian (pen-and-paper learning journal), taught in an Australian university. Participants were 29 students who studied French and 34 students who studied Italian. Qualitative and quantitative methods were used to analyse the data collected with the use of an online SurveyMonkey questionnaire. The author highlights the fact that FA reflective tasks are not often used in tertiary education. The findings of this process-oriented, formative approach to assessment, fulfilled through regular engagement with classwork and the target language and teacher's close monitoring of students' work, revealed that reflective tasks (blogs, diaries) can engage students and offer more opportunities for using the target language. However, they revealed that students preferred to reflect individually (reflective journal) rather than collectively (the blog). The value of the source lies in its contribution to the general discussion of the value of reflective tasks as FA practices in LL at tertiary level.

Erdogan, T., & Yurdabakan, I. (2011). Secondary school students' opinions on portfolio assessment in EFL. *International Journal on New Trends in Education and Their Implications, 2*(3), 63-72.

> This experimental study, published in a peer-reviewed journal, identifies secondary students' views of portfolios as FA practices in an EFL learning context in Turkey. Participants were 22 secondary students from a state secondary school of Izmir. There were ten open-ended questions about students' opinions on PA; the questions were reviewed by experts. The responses of students were analysed by using content analysis. The findings showed some positive and some negative outcomes. On the one hand, participants found portfolios as a fair procedure and an increase in responsibility of students. On the other hand, however, students felt that the reading part of the portfolio, the self-evaluation, and the homework were hard. Also, according to students' responses, portfolios can be considered as a more realistic approach compared to traditional testing applications. In this article, more research tools could have been used in order to analyse the data and enhance the reliability and validity of the research. This source highlights the use of portfolios as an FA tool.

Graham, S., Harris, K. R., & Hebert, M. A. (2011). *Informing writing: the benefits of formative assessment. A Carnegie Corporation Time to Act Report.* Alliance for Excellence in Education. https://www.carnegie.org/publications/informing-writing-the-benefits-of-formative-assessment/

> This report from the US discusses if FA practices can improve students' writing skills and how teachers can improve writing assessment in the classroom. It is claimed by the author that this was the first report that used meta-analysis to highlight the role of FA writing. It describes some FA writing practices, like teaching students how to assess their own writing. The findings showed that FA for writing purposes improved students' writing skills with the involvement of teachers and peers. Also, it was suggested by the authors that teachers could use 21st

century writing tools and be well-prepared for their lessons. While this report is referring to benefits of FA in writing in general, it also provides significant guidelines for FA implementations for L2 instructors in particular.

Heritage, M., & Chang, S. (2012). Teacher use of formative assessment data for English language learners. *National Centre for Research on Evaluation, Standards, & Student Testing*. https://cresst.org/wp-content/uploads/ELL_Symposium_FINAL.pdf

This article is an exploratory analysis on teachers' feedback in online reports to ELL on reading assessments in a US context. This analysis was part of a bigger project for FA and ELL students, which was conducted by the ETS, in collaboration with CRESST at the University of California, Los Angeles. The participants were 11 middle-school teachers in the focus groups, and eight of them completed the teacher survey. The teachers were from urban and suburban areas of New Jersey, California, and Wisconsin. Transcripts and open-ended survey responses were qualitatively coded. The findings revealed that teachers did not have a clear idea of the purpose of using FA; according to the authors, this could be explained by the fact that many teachers focused more on summative assessment practices. As in many other articles, this study confirms findings from earlier studies, which support that the language educators do not fully understand the purpose of implementing FA practices in their teaching, and that appropriate training in FA in LL is required.

Carreira, M. M. (2012). Formative assessment in HL teaching: purposes, procedures, and practices. *Heritage Language Journal*, *9*(1), 100-120. https://doi.org/10.46538/hlj.9.1.6

This peer-reviewed article focuses on FA as a tool to deal with students' diverse problems in heritage language classes in a North American context. It is stated in the article that many FA tools like journals, portfolios, and quizzes can be used to provide information to teachers about learners' performances. This paper describes the implementation of FA applications in a Spanish course, which is the first of two Heritage LL courses at California State University, Long Beach. The findings of this paper highlight the significance of the diagnostic aspect of FA, especially for placement purposes. Also, as the author mentions, FA is considered the best path to lead to SA. The number of studies found and included in this AB related to FA practices in heritage language classes is limited. The value of the source lies in the fact that it fills some of the gap in this under-researched area.

Huang, S. C. (2012). Like a bell responding to a striker: instruction contingent on assessment. *English Teaching: Practice and Critique, 11*(4), 99-119. https://files.eric.ed.gov/fulltext/EJ999757.pdf

This peer-reviewed article is about the role of AFL in higher quality learning in the day-to-day classroom. The article consists of two parts. The first part is a review of the recent studies within Black and Wiliam's (2009) framework of FA. The second part is a description of an instructional design contingent on FA, based on the lessons learnt from the review of those studies. The author then describes the L2 writing lesson designed based on AFL principles and implemented in the fall 2011 semester in Taiwan, as part of an integrated-skill freshman English course. The data analysis from the results collected with the use of an online questionnaire revealed that, among the 107 students, 61 participated in the survey and were generally quite positive about their learning experience. The author concluded that one should be aware that this type of teaching demands a great deal more from teachers. The first part of the article can be considered a good review of the research conducted in the area. The second part is equally important as it contributes to this research with further findings.

Karagianni, E. (2012). Employing computer assisted assessment (CAA) to facilitate formative assessment in the State Secondary School: a case study.

Research Papers in Language Teaching and Learning, 3(1), 252-268. http://rpltl.eap.gr/images/2012/03-01-252-Karagianni.pdf

> This peer-reviewed research paper presents a case study conducted in Greece which discusses the integration of CAA for FA in an EFL learning context in Greek public schools. The participants were 25 14-year-old students, ten boys and 15 girls. Data were collected through questionnaires, quizzes like Hot Potatoes, and self-questionnaires. The findings showed that computers can be effective tools for FA and that this can be very beneficial for EFL students and teachers. Also, according to the findings, students' grammar improved. This paper adds to the existing discussion of the use of technologies in FA LL.

Muñoz, A. P., Palacio, M., & Escobar, L. (2012). Teachers' beliefs about assessment in an EFL context in Colombia. *Profile Issues in Teachers Professional Development, 14*(1), 143-158. https://revistas.unal.edu.co/index.php/profile/article/view/29064

> This peer-reviewed article presents a study from Colombia which presents teachers' perceptions on EFL assessment. The participants were 62 EFL teachers in a private university in Colombia. A mixed-methods approach was utilised incorporating surveys, interviews, and a written report of experiences. The survey was analysed using descriptive statistics. Then all data were triangulated in order to ensure validity and reliability. Results showed that there is a discrepancy between teachers' assessment practices and teachers' beliefs. Teachers believed that assessment should be more FA but in action, they followed more SA practices. The study indicates the need for further investigation of the reason for this discrepancy that exists in many countries, and calls for more teacher training in FA in LL.

Tabatabaei, O., & Assefi, F. (2012). The effect of portfolio assessment technique on writing performance of EFL learners. *English Language Teaching, 5*(5), 138-147. https://doi.org/10.5539/elt.v5n5p138

This peer-reviewed article explores the formative potential of portfolio assessment and the impact of the use of portfolios on EFL learners in a writing context in Iran. The participants were 40 English teaching major students. These students were divided into two groups of 20 learners each, an experimental group and a control group. All participants took TOEFL and standardised IELTS writing to ensure homogeneity of their writing ability. The portfolio model that was used was based on the classroom portfolio model and consisted of three procedures: collection, selection, and reflection. An analytic scoring was also implemented. The findings showed that the use of portfolios for FA purposes had a positive impact on students' writing abilities. The students of the experimental group who experienced the use of portfolios for FA purposes outperformed the students of the control group who encountered traditional writing assessments. This study confirmed earlier studies and contributed its own findings indicating the benefits of the use of portfolios for FA purposes.

Tang, J., Rich, C. S., & Wang, Y. (2012). Technology-enhanced English language writing assessment in the classroom. *Chinese Journal of Applied Linguistics,* 35(4), 385-399.

This fully refereed article reports on a pilot study as part of a three-year research project funded by China's Ministry of Education to investigate the implementation of technology-enhanced FA in the classroom. The study took place in nine primary and three junior high schools in China. The total number of participants were 1,243 students and were separated into an experimental and a control group. The large number of participants in this study increased the validity and reliability of the findings. A mixed-method was implemented. Questionnaires, journals, quasi-experimental pre- and post-tests were used to collect data. The initial pilot study findings showed that most students had a positive attitude toward the use of an automated assessment writing tool such as WRM. Students became more autonomous, motivated, and confident in their writing with the use of WRM, and teachers switched from a traditional instructor role to that of a supporter and facilitator. However, the study also revealed the need to further explain the marking system of WRM to both students and teachers.

Babaee, M., & Tikoduadua, M. (2013). E-portfolios: a new trend in formative writing assessment. *International Journal of Modern Education Forum (IJMEF)*, *2*(2), 49-56.

This peer-reviewed article from Australia presents the impact of alternative assessment strategies in writing. It focuses on e-portfolios as a new trend in formative writing assessment for EFL and ESL learners. It highlights the advantages and challenges of e-portfolio based FA. It is argued by the authors that the use of portfolios as an FA tool encourages self-regulation, reflection, and autonomy. In this source, it is also stated that portfolio assessment encourages the use of social media in education. Another benefit of e-portfolio mentioned was that it offers drafting, editing, and revising advantages. Furthermore, the authors argued that social networks and e-portfolios can promote peer assessment and self-assessment. This article contributes to the discussion of the use of e-portfolios for FA purposes.

Chen, Q., Kettle, M., Klenowski, V., & May, L. (2013). Interpretations of formative assessment in the teaching of English at two Chinese universities: a sociocultural perspective. *Assessment & Evaluation in Higher Education*, *38*(7), 831-846. https://doi.org/10.1080/02602938.2012.726963

This peer-reviewed article reports on a research study which investigated how two Chinese universities (an urban and a regional) interpreted FA in college English teaching. The participants were five female and two male English teachers. A qualitative case study was used with interviews with teachers and administrators as research tools to obtain data. Both universities had used FA practices. The findings from the two universities revealed that they shared the same interpretations of FA on process and student participation. Their differences related to the specific sociocultural conditions, socioeconomic status, and teacher and student roles, expectations, and beliefs about English. The findings illustrated the challenge of implementing FA in a Chinese context, historically oriented to summative assessment, as it was originally conceptualised in Western contexts.

Haines, K., Meima, E., & Faber, M. (2013). Formative assessment and the support of lecturers in the international university. In *International Experiences in Language Testing and Assessment* (pp. 177-190). Peter Lang.

This peer-reviewed chapter presents case studies from the Netherlands with FA implementations and 'person-in context'. The research has followed a qualitative research method and used LanQua to evaluate the procedures that were implemented. This chapter highlights some issues at the tertiary level in the Netherlands. It is about the fact that many lecturers who are non-native speakers of English must deliver their lectures in English and these instructors need to be assessed. However, the Language Centre of the University of Groningen decided to assess their academics by adapting FA practices based on authentic context and related to working experiences in the university context. The LanQua Quality Model was used as a foundation to support the lecturers. In addition to this, the person-in context principle was incorporated to identify the real-life needs and priorities of academics in their university life in two faculties at the University of Groningen, the Faculty of Social Sciences, and the Faculty of Medical Sciences. The findings revealed that the lecturers felt that FA implementations with the provision of meaningful feedback and the construction of portfolios made them more confident for their lectures in English. This chapter adds a different dimension to the discussion of the use of FA in LL, that of the FA assessment of academics who are non-native speakers of English and who deliver their lectures in English.

Restrepo, A., & Nelson, H. (2013). Role of systematic formative assessment on students' views of their learning. *Profile Issues in Teachers Professional*

Development, 15(2), 165-183. http://www.scielo.org.co/scielo.php?pid=S1657-07902013000200011&script=sci_arttext&tlng=pt

> This peer-reviewed article presents students' views during and after FA implementations (feedback, self-assessment, conferences, role play) in a public university in Medellin in Colombia. The participants were nine English beginner learners (three male and six female) aged from 18 to 40. The author used a qualitative exploratory, descriptive, and interpretive research method. The data were collected through observations and interviews. The findings showed that FA enables students to autonomously identify their own strengths and weaknesses, and critical reflections on their own learning, and to acquire an awareness of their own communicative skills. The findings also revealed the benefits of FA which goes beyond grading and attempts to understand students' learning from the teacher's and the learners' point of view, which gathers information that benefits their learning and eventually leads to a more accurate summative assessment. This article focuses on another dimension of the use of FA in LL, that of students' views of FA.

Tsagari, D., & Michaeloudes, G. (2013). Formative assessment patterns in CLIL primary schools in Cyprus. In S. Ioannou-Georgiou, S. Papadima-Sophocleous & D. Tsagari (Eds), *International experiences in language testing and assessment* (pp. 75-93). Peter Lang Edition.

> This peer-reviewed chapter presents research on how FA was implemented in a CLIL pilot programme in primary schools of the Republic of Cyprus. This study explored the nature of CLIL which includes the incorporation of the subject content and the use of FL. It presents different types of FA in CLIL teaching with the use of FL. Qualitative and quantitative methods were used to collect data. Questionnaires were given to three female CLIL teachers. Observations were also used to collect more information. Five lessons were observed and audio-recorded. Results indicated that teachers prioritised content

over the FL. The most common types of FA used by teachers was questioning, and the initiation-response-feedback pattern. The authors concluded that the implementation of CLIL was an initiative step in Cyprus and a limited number of teachers used it. They suggested that more observations of CLIL lessons could give a more valid outcome of FA implementations within CLIL. The authors recommended that teachers in Cyprus should be trained in courses that combine FA strategies with CLIL. The research gives insights into the use of FA in CLIL contexts and highlights the necessity of teacher training.

Shin, S. Y. (2013). Developing a framework for using e-portfolios as a research and assessment tool. *ReCALL*, *25*(3), 359-372. https://doi.org/10.1017/S0958344013000189

This peer-reviewed article from the US supports that e-portfolios can serve as a valuable research and assessment tool for collecting and storing an individual learner's language samples obtained across different tasks over time. In that way, e-portfolios can address the limitation of data access which prohibits the understanding of individual developmental trends in interlanguage as well as the interpretation of context effects on the learner's spoken and written language data. According to the author, e-portfolios can include multimedia input and constructed response tasks in order to enhance the situational and interactional authenticity of tasks. At the same time, the author addresses some limitations that e-portfolios may have. For example, how tasks in them can be constructed to represent various linguistics and situational contexts, and how they could be systematically evaluated and scored. Further discussion on limitations and on recommendations for future research is included. One of the recommendations is the provision of a framework for systematic evaluation, particularly when e-portfolios are intended to be used as an FA instrument.

Tuttle, H. G., & Tuttle, A. (2013). *Improving foreign language speaking through formative assessment*. Routledge. https://doi.org/10.4324/9781315854854

Part 3

> This publication from the US provides detailed information and suggestions to language teachers on how they can use FA practices to improve their students' speaking skills. The book consists of three parts: Part 1 is related to speaking assessment and improvement. Part 2 is an overview of FA. Part 3 is about speaking FAs. The book gives an overview of FA with explanations on how to engage students in self and peer assessment. It also provides examples with lesson plans of FA implementations aligned to ACTFL guidelines. The authors believe that if teachers apply more FA strategies in their teaching, students can learn an FL in six to seven months. This book can be considered as a useful guide to teachers for L2 FA practices.

Rezaee, A. A., Alavi, S. M., & Shabani, E. A. (2013). Alternative assessment or traditional testing: how do Iranian EFL teachers respond? *Teaching English Language, 7*(2), 151-190. https://doi.org/10.22132/TEL.2013.54864

> This peer-reviewed article explores Iranian teachers' attitudes towards alternative and traditional assessment and investigates their ethical views on language testing. The qualitative research method was used to collect data through a questionnaire that was shared online to a big number (N=326) of adult EFL teachers in Iran. It was completed by 153 teachers. Semi-structured individual interviews with open-ended questions were also administered. The findings revealed that a larger number of respondents claimed that traditional testing and alternative assessment (which, according to Alderson & Banerjee, 2001, is usually formative rather than summative in function) are both necessary. It was also clear from their responses that formal traditional testing was more commonly used than alternative types of assessment like portfolio and reflections. Moreover, no respondent admitted that ethical issues were related to language testing and assessment. Added to that, all teachers agreed that alternative assessment implementations should be carried out at all levels of education; primary, secondary, and higher. This article reinforces earlier research which supports that alternative assessments do not replace summative assessment but work more as supplementary

tools. The particular value of this article lies in the large number of participants which enhances the validity and reliability of the research outcomes.

Alvarez, L., Ananda, S., Walqui, A., Sato, E., & Rabinowitz, S. (2014). *Focusing formative assessment on the needs of English language learners.* https://www.wested.org/wp-content/uploads/2016/11/1391626953FormativeAssessment_report5-3.pdf

This paper is one in a series produced by WestEd (US) on the topic of FA. It examines the importance of FA to ELL primary students. According to the authors, not much research has been conducted with innovating FA strategies for ELL students. ELL students are considered the students who are not proficient in English yet and need more support in their class work. In the US, the population of ELL students is growing to 5.3 million. In this paper, an FA approach to ELL students is recommended based on: (1) articulation of the construct being taught and assessed, (2) elicitation of evidence about ELL students' learning, and (3) interpretation of data. It is also stated that FA can help students to learn other teaching subjects and at the same time learn English. The authors also provide suggestions on how schools can be supported to incorporate FA strategies for ELL students. This paper can be a useful guideline to school administrators, and L2 teachers to ELL students.

Burner, T. (2014). The potential formative benefits of portfolio assessment in second and foreign language writing contexts: a review of the literature. *Studies in Educational Evaluation, 43,* 139-149. https://doi.org/10.1016/j.stueduc.2014.03.002

This peer-reviewed article originating from Norway is a literature review on the benefits of PA as a type of FA in L2/FL classrooms. It is based on database search, manual search, and citation search resulting in a total of 39 peer-reviewed articles, between November 2012 and

October 2013. According to the findings, the advantages of using a PA are the authenticity and interactivity, the development of motivation, learner autonomy, and the improvement of writing skills. However, the author suggests that more empirical studies should be conducted in FA areas especially in primary and secondary education. This is a valuable contribution that highlights PA as a significant FA tool during the specific period of time, for those interested in the potential formative benefits of portfolio assessment in L2/FL writing, and a good example for similar research in other aspects of FA in LL.

Cho, S., & Park, C. (2014). The role of scoring in formative assessment of second language writing. *GEMA Online® Journal of Language Studies, 14*(3). https://doi.org/10.17576/GEMA-2014-1403-07

This referred article from South Korea examines the impact of scoring in FA of L2 writing. The participants were 32 first-year college students. They were divided into two classes: the one class was receiving scoring and written feedback on each paper, and the second one was receiving only feedback. A mixed-method was applied with statistical analysis and interviews, and the writing assignments of four students were compared. The findings showed that the students in the scoring group had a better awareness of their writings. As a response to earlier research which reported negative effects of scoring on learning and teaching, this study suggests that scoring can encourage learners to become more fully responsible for their learning and can result in more and better learning.

Chen, Q., May, L., Klenowski, V., & Kettle, M. (2014). The enactment of formative assessment in English language classrooms in two Chinese universities: teacher and student responses. *Assessment in Education: Principles, Policy & Practice, 21*(3), 271-285. https://doi.org/10.1080/0969594X.2013.790308

This peer-reviewed article discusses the enactment of FA in teaching and learning English by the Chinese Ministry of Education in 2007. The

College of English Curriculum Requirements suggest the integration of FA for English LL. Researchers used a case study to examine the changes of enactment in two Chinese universities, a key university from the national capital and a non-key university from the Western province. Two instructors took part in this research. This study was based on lessons' observations and interviews with teachers and learners. The students' participation in different types of FA was analysed in both universities. The main focus was on providing feedback. The findings showed that students were reluctant to use FA practices and especially peer assessment because they were sceptical of their usefulness. This reflected the reluctance to introduce, adopt, and implement assessment practices originally intended for other contexts to Chinese contexts. This article adds to the research exploring the perceptions of students and teachers regarding FA in LL. It also brings to light the importance of adequate training to both teachers and students when new practices are introduced.

Jiang, Y. (2014). Exploring teacher questioning as a formative assessment strategy. *RELC Journal*, *45*(3), 287-304. https://doi.org/10.1177/0033688214546962

This peer-reviewed article investigates EFL teachers' questioning as a type of FA implementation in two Chinese tertiary institutions in the People's Republic of China. The paper emphasises on teachers' questions as a strategy to challenge students and stimulate their critical thinking. Moreover, it offers examples of questioning as a type of FA. According to the findings, teachers' questions can benefit students. Emphasis is made on the role of teachers' questioning as a type of FA can stimulate students' motivation and awareness on learning. This article offers new knowledge to the use of questioning as FA in LL and may instigate interest in further research in the area.

Jian, H., & Luo, S. (2014). Formative assessment in L2 classroom in China: the current situation, predicament and future. *Indonesian Journal of Applied Linguistics*, *3*(2), 18-34. https://doi.org/10.17509/ijal.v3i2.266

> This peer-reviewed article describes the FA development in L2 classroom practices in China from 2001 to 2012. It includes 1,959 articles, four monographs, and three PhD dissertations. A mixed-methods approach was used for this research. Although the reform of English education in China since 2001 helped FA find its way into key educational policy documents, the findings revealed that FA in China is not sufficiently researched (less than 2,000 publications) and not implemented to a great extent. Also, results indicated that the level of FA understanding of teachers and institutions was very low. Moreover, the authors found that the main reason for the low understanding of FA in China was the low financial support, inadequate research in FA implementations, and the dominance of testing. This article stresses the importance of these elements in the introduction of new concepts and practices such as FA in LL.

Ketabi, S., & Ketabi, S. (2014). Classroom and formative assessment in second/ foreign language teaching and learning. *Theory & Practice in Language Studies*, *4*(2), 435-440. https://doi.org/10.4304/tpls.4.2.435-440

> This peer-reviewed article written by researchers from the University of Isfahan in Iran, describes different types of assessment. It compares FA and classroom assessment, FA and SA, formal and informal assessment, and explicit and implicit assessment. The authors report on the effects of FA in ESL/EFL teaching and learning and they suggest that teachers should make their classroom assessment more formative. This research can be considered as a useful guide for FA practices in language teaching and learning.

Öz, H. (2014). Turkish teachers' practices of assessment for learning in the English as a foreign language classroom. *Journal of Language Teaching & Research*, *5*(4). https://doi.org/10.4304/jltr.5.4.775-785

> This peer-reviewed article investigates assessment practices, and more specifically FA practices of EFL teachers. As the author states,

this study aimed to fill in the gap of identifying teachers 'perceptions on assessment practices in Turkey'. The participants were 120 EFL teachers teaching in both public and private educational institutions. The data were collected through an online questionnaire, which was shared via a social networking service. The data were analysed with the use of IBM SPSS Statistics 2 and descriptive statistics. The findings showed that most Turkish EFL teachers used conventional methods of assessment rather than FA ones. Moreover, they considered formal examinations as the only form of assessment they can rely on. This finding supports the claims made in earlier studies that Turkey is still an exam-oriented country, and that teachers need to be supported in developing knowledge, skills, and experiences in FA in LL. This study is an important contribution, as the context described is widely relatable, and the insights provided are important for the development of FA in language education.

Smith, D. H., & Davis, J. E. (2014). Formative assessment for student progress and programme improvement in sign language as L2 programmes. In D. McKee, R. S. Rosen & R. McKee (Eds), *Teaching and learning signed languages* (pp. 253-280). Palgrave Macmillan. https://doi.org/10.1057/9781137312495_12

This book chapter from the US provides a literature review on Sign Language and focuses on the contribution of FA in Sign Language as an L2. It focuses on the effective role of feedback for evaluating Sign Language in L2 programmes. It investigates the efficacy of an online FA tool in a Sign Language programme at the tertiary level in the US. The authors concluded that more assessment tools are needed for L2 Sign Language learners and more research should be conducted with a larger number of participants. This publication is of special value as it is the only one found during our research that focuses on FA in L2 Sign Language.

Wolf, M. K., Shore, J. R., & Blood, I. (2014). *English learner formative assessment (ELFA): a design framework*. ETS. https://www.ets.org/s/research/pdf/elfa_design_framework.pdf

Part 3

> This research project was designed by researchers and assessment developers at ETS in collaboration with research partners at the CRESST at UCLA. Its aim was to provide an important guideline to help their students to improve their reading skills. Examples of different strategies and activities for FA purposes were presented. Moreover, users of ELFA were advised to have a look at the teacher's guide, and the teacher's versions to have a better understanding of FA. It can be stated that it gives a better understanding to teachers of examples of FA implementations. It was designed to be used in classes for ESL, ELD, or ELA lessons. This publication can be considered as a useful guideline for English language teachers if they desire to implement FA strategies for reading skills. It could also provide a better understanding of the ELFA Design Framework and how it could be used for formative purposes for both assessment developers and assessment users.

Radford, B. W. (2014). *The effect of formative assessments on languageperformance*. Unpublished doctoral dissertation. Brigham Young, Provo. http://scholarsarchive.byu.edu/etd/3978

> This PhD dissertation explores the improvements of FA implementations on language performance at the Missionary Training Centre in Provo, Utah, US. The researcher's hypothesis was that the use of FA strategies and instant feedback would increase learning outcomes. For this purpose, computer-based practices were used. The 128 participants were randomly selected and aged from 19-24. Participants were learning Spanish as an L2. The research method was based on two by two factorial designs. The findings revealed that teaching of language performance criteria improves speaking skills. Moreover, it was suggested that students benefitted from receiving computer formative feedback. This source highlights the effect of a technology-enhanced environment for LL FA purposes.

Zhao, H. (2014). Investigating teacher-supported peer assessment for EFL writing. *ELT Journal, 68*(2), 155-168. https://doi.org/10.1093/elt/cct068

This peer-reviewed article investigates the impact of teacher-supported assessment for EFL writing, viewed as a formative developmental process that gives writers the opportunity to discuss their texts and discover others' interpretations of them (Hyland, 2000). The participants were 18 second-year English major university students in China. The teacher trained students in how to provide constructive feedback to their peers for their writing. The data were collected through a pre-assessment survey and a post-assessment survey of students. The findings from the post-assessment survey showed that all students were satisfied with the teacher support strategies. Also, students' training by the teacher improved the efficiency of peer assessment. This article contributes to the discussion of feedback as FA practice, with the emphasis it gives on the importance of training students on how to provide effective feedback.

Hansson, S. (2015). *Benefits and difficulties in using peer response for writing in the EFL classroom.* Göteborgs Universitet. https://gupea.ub.gu.se/bitstream/2077/38436/1/gupea_2077_38436_1.pdf

This text discusses the benefits and difficulties in implementing peer assessment in writing EFL classrooms as a form of FA by reviewing articles and books. It is mentioned that peer response is considered important by the curriculum in Sweden but the question is how much and how it is used, and if it is used efficiently. The report presents some benefits of using peer response by providing the positive outcomes of many researches, like increase of students' awareness, self-regulation, self-motivation, and feeling less anxiety. Also, some considerations and difficulties when applying peer assessment were discussed. These involved not trusting their peers' feedback; the teachers' comments were more appreciated than their peers; issues of friendship bias. Moreover, some suggestions were included and these report the necessity of creating a comfortable environment for teachers when it is time for peer assessment. Also, students can create their own assessment criteria and can be trained on how to give peer

> response. This publication can be a useful guideline in peer-assessing for LL FA purposes.

Herrera L., & Macías, D. F. (2015). A call for language assessment literacy in the education and development of teachers of English as a foreign language. *Colombian Applied Linguistics Journal, 17*(2), 302-312. https://doi.org/10.14483/udistrital.jour.calj.2015.2.a09

> This peer-reviewed article aims to raise awareness for more preparation in assessment for language teachers, including EFL teachers in Colombia. The article provides a number of definitions of LAL. It reviews some studies that are related to LAL. The authors discuss assessment literacy and its relevance for EFL teaching, and consider what constitutes the knowledge base of language assessment. Their review found various studies which addressed LAL; however, they stress the need for more research in the area. They support Stiggins's (2007) claim that since "teachers spend as much as one-quarter to one-third of their available professional time in assessment-related activities", their assessment teacher preparation should receive the same importance as that of instruction. LAL teacher education should balance both classroom (which also includes FA) and accountability assessments (e.g. large-scale standardised tests). Language teacher education programmes should include alternatives and should constitute part of teachers' lifelong learning. Alternatives of LAL acquisition can be workshops, conferences, independent readings, study groups, collaborative action research, and projects. The authors also believe that language assessment should be informed by their immediate context. Their contribution is their call for the importance of LAL in EFL teacher education, which includes FA, and their recommendations towards the development of LAL among EFL teachers.

Kuo, C. L. (2015). *A quasi-experimental study of formative peer assessment in an EFL writing classroom.* Unpublished doctoral dissertation. Newcastle University. http://theses.ncl.ac.uk/jspui/handle/10443/2863

This PhD dissertation is a quasi-experimental study, which investigates the impact of 'Step Training' proposed by Min in peer assessment of an EFL writing classroom in Taiwan. The author states that peer assessment is theoretically based on four learning stances: process writing theory, collaborative learning theory, Vygoskty's ZPD, and interaction and L2 acquisition. The participants were 127 students and two teachers from the W College of Languages (pseudonym) of Taiwan. They were separated into two groups, an experimental and a control group. A mixed-method approach was followed. The data were collected through questionnaires, video recordings, and interviews, and data were analysed with the use of ANCOVA analysis. The findings showed that students from the experimental group (who had training in peer assessment) produced higher quality feedback than the students from the control group who did not receive any training. The author suggests that negotiation is very important for the student so that the student could have the opportunity to create their own identity in the peer assessment procedure. This research contributes to the discussion of the importance of training students in applying peer assessment practices.

Lazzeri, S., Cabezas, X., Ojeda, L., & Leiva, F. (2015). Automated formative evaluations for reading comprehension in an English as a foreign language course: benefits on performance, user satisfaction, and monitoring of higher education students in Chile. In F. Helm, L. Bradley, M. Guarda & S. Thouësny (Eds), *CriticalCALL – proceedings of the 2015 EUROCALL Conference*, Padova, Italy (pp. 355-361). Research-publishing.net. https://doi.org/10.14705/rpnet.2015.000358

This conference proceedings paper reports on the implementation of the tool QMP in a Chilean context. This tool was used by the students of the University Kinesiology who studied ESP. The researchers implemented QMP to investigate if the automated formative evaluations used improved students' reading comprehension skills. The researchers of this study used experiment design with a pre-test and a post-test for two groups, an experimental and a control group (G1 and G2). The results from the pre-test and post-tests of the two groups indicated no significant difference. However, students from the G1 experimental group showed positive attitudes experiencing the implementation of QMP and researchers suggested that technology applications should be used more often for formative purposes. This paper contributes to the research conducted in the use of technology in FA in LL.

Lam, R. (2015). Language assessment training in Hong Kong: implications for language assessment literacy. *Language Testing, 32*(2), 169-197. https://doi.org/10.1177/0265532214554321

This peer-reviewed article investigates the language assessment training area in five Hong Kong teacher education institutions during assessment reforms in primary/secondary school contexts; more specifically, the research dealt with how two language assessment courses supported pre-service teachers to acquire LAL. The participants were nine instructors and 40 pre-service teachers studying in the final year. The study was based on qualitative research. The data were collected with the use of interviews, teaching evaluations, student assessment tasks, and government documents. For the purposes of this research, the author researched all undergraduate programmes in ELT by using the SCOLAR website, which embodied all the recognised language degree programmes. The findings revealed that language assessment training in Hong Kong is still insufficient. The author suggests improvement through updating their purpose, content, delivery, and overall quality. The author stressed the need to equip pre-service teachers with fundamental knowledge, skills, and principles in handling both large-scale and classroom-based FAs and enable them to learn how to use them for the benefit of student learning through continuous professional learning. Moreover, the author provided some suggestions for the implications of LAL. This study emphasises the role of teachers' training for L2 FA purposes.

Levy, T., & Gertler, H. (2015). Harnessing technology to assess oral communication in Business English. *Teaching English with Technology*, *15*(4), 52-59. https://files.eric.ed.gov/fulltext/EJ1138436.pdf

> This peer-reviewed article presents an action research which argues that the use of digital tools can increase students' motivation and engagement in learning business English for oral and communication skills. It also claims that FA and teacher's feedback helped students improve their work, although this was not substantiated clearly enough. The research took place in a public college for business administration in Israel. Students ranged from 21-35 year-olds. They had to pass the ESP course in order to receive their degree. This action research paper was based on observations. For FA purposes, a rubric was given to students to know how they would be graded and online tools like Socrative, Kahoot, Mailvu, Movenote, and Vidme were also used. Digital tools enabled lecturers to assess students' progress continuously and give feedback. All students passed their exams. Although this course was focused on business English, it has been claimed that it could be applied to different language courses.

Titova, S. (2015). Use of mobile testing system PeLe for developing language skills. In F. Helm, L. Bradley, M. Guarda & S. Thouësny (Eds), *Critical CALL – proceedings of the 2015 EUROCALL Conference* (pp. 523-528). Research-publishing.net. https://doi.org/10.14705/rpnet.2015.000387

> This conference proceedings reviewed paper from Russia explores the intervention of the mobile testing system PeLe (eight tests) as FA tools for practising language skills. This research was first piloted as part of the research project MobiLL in Lomonosov Moscow State University and the Norwegian University College. The data were collected through qualitative and quantitative research methods. The participants were 35 students in preparatory English courses. Two control groups were tested by pen-and-paper traditional tests and two experimental groups took the PeLe tests on grammar and vocabulary tests. The findings revealed that

students benefited from the PeLe mobile testing system, which could be sampled in other courses as well.

Bachelor, J. W., & Bachelor, R. B. (2016). Classroom currency as a means of formative feedback, reflection, and assessment in the world language classroom. *NECTFL Review, 78*, 31-42. https://files.eric.ed.gov/fulltext/EJ1256488.pdf

This reviewed conference paper article presents an American study that investigates the role of FA types: formative feedback, reflections, and rubrics in the World Language Community College classroom. The participants were 57 students from three sections of Elementary Spanish I of a community college in the Midwest of the United States during the fall of 2015. The students used a reward play money system where they had to reward the teacher when they achieved daily goals or learning objectives. The data from the students' feedback to the instructor and the instructor rubric indicated the students' preferences of communicative activities, and revealed that students performed well based on the instructor FA. The reward play money system is mentioned only in this study in the whole of this AB. This research can instigate further interest in this area.

Bahati, B., Tedre, M., Fors, U., & Evode, M. (2016). Exploring feedback practises in formative assessment in Rwandan higher education: a multifaceted approach is needed. *International Journal of Teaching and Education, 4*(2), 1-22. https://doi.org/10.20472/TE.2016.4.2.001

This peer-reviewed article describes the role of feedback in FA at the University of Rwanda. Eight lecturers and 75 university students took part in this research. Qualitative methods were used through semi-structured lecturers' and students' interviews and focus group discussions. The results indicated that feedback was only provided in the sense of marks and grades by lecturers. The lecturers saw themselves as the main source of providing information and had all the responsibility of what they portrayed as FA. According to students' responses in interviews, feedback was ineffective and useless, because it was delayed at the end of the semester or exams' period. The author suggested that if feedback was delivered on time, it would be effective. He also recommended a multifaceted collaborative approach with researchers, students, and decision makers involved in FA and feedback practices. Although this article is about FA and feedback, it is indicative of the fact that there is a need to further clarify various terms such as FA and feedback in order to be able to use them as appropriately as possible in both assessment practices and in research.

Burner, T. (2016). Formative assessment of writing in English as a foreign language. *Scandinavian Journal of Educational Research, 60*(6), 626-648. https://doi.org/10.1080/00313831.2015.1066430

This peer-reviewed article is a mixed-method study conducted in Norway, which investigates the integration of FA in EFL with the main focus on writing skills. The participants were four teachers and 100 learners from eighth and ninth grade. Research tools included a questionnaire, and a case survey. The findings revealed that many contradictions arose from teachers and students' insights in FA implementations. These contradictions were related to feedback, self-assessment, grades, and students' participation. Moreover, the authors concluded that it is necessary for teachers and students to have a deeper understanding of FA implementations, like many other articles in this AB, which stresses the importance of teachers' and students' clearer understanding of the characteristics of FA.

Crusan, D., Plakans, L., & Gebril, A. (2016). Writing assessment literacy: surveying second language teachers' knowledge, beliefs, and practices. *Assessing Writing, 28,* 43-56. https://doi.org/10.1016/j.asw.2016.03.001

In this refereed article, the authors present research which focuses on teachers' L2 assessment literacy (knowledge, beliefs, practices) in an American context. A large number of 702 L2 instructors from tertiary institutions participated in the research. The data were collected through Survey Monkey questionnaires, using multiple-choice, Likert scale, and open-ended response items. Four questions were the main focus of this research.

- "How have L2 writing teachers obtained assessment knowledge"?
- "What do L2 writing teachers believe about writing assessment"?
- "What are the assessment practices of L2 writing teachers"?
- "What is the impact of linguistic background and teaching experience on writing assessment knowledge, beliefs, and practises"?

The findings revealed that only 26% of the teachers had little or no training on writing assessment. However, while there was evidence that teachers received training in writing assessment, it was also revealed that a number of teachers were not clear about what that entailed. Moreover, it was mentioned that teachers did not have a clear idea about the differences between formative and summative assessment. Like many other articles in this AB, this article stresses the need for a clearer understanding by teachers of what FA entails.

Estaji, M., & Fassihi, S. (2016). On the relationship between the implementation of formative assessment strategies and Iranian EFL teachers' self-efficacy: do gender and experience make a difference? *Journal of English Language Teaching and Learning, 8*(18), 65-86. https://elt.tabrizu.ac.ir/article_5494.html

This double-blind peer-reviewed article examines the relationship between the use of FA strategies of EFL teachers, their gender, level of experience, and sense of self-efficacy. The participants were 61 EFL teachers (31 female and 30 male teachers); all of them held a Master's degree and were teaching English at different English language institutes in Tehran, Iran. Multiple statistical strategies were used to analyse the data. A three-way ANOVA was run so as to scrutinise the interaction between the use of FA strategies, EFL teachers' gender, level of experience, and their self-efficacy. The results showed that there was no statistically significant interaction between the teachers' use of FA strategies, teachers' sense of self-efficacy, their gender, and level of experience. The authors suggested that future research should be conducted to investigate the role of teachers' use of FA strategies on the learners' language skills. This article explores areas of FA, which have not extensively been examined yet.

Joo, S. H. (2016). Self and peer assessment of speaking. *Studies in Applied Linguistics and TESOL*, *16*(2). https://doi.org/10.7916/salt.v16i2.1257

This double-blind peer-reviewed article, written by an author teaching in South Korea, explores the learners' abilities to assess their own and their peers' oral performances and the factors in self- and peer-assessment that affect the enhancement of L2 speaking ability. The multiple dimensions of LOA are reviewed and used by the author as a guiding framework to conduct the research. According to the author, some factors that affect the learning process are sociocognitive, affective, interactional, and some other contextual variables. Moreover, it is mentioned that there is a strong interaction between peer and self-assessment with a technology-assisted environment. The article concludes that if the relevant conditions are met, then the learners would be able to assess themselves or others. These conditions are related to sufficient training, clear provision of task-related criteria, and considerations of the learners' traits and their perceptions. The value of the source lies in the fact that it emphasises the importance of students' training.

Huang, S. C. (2016). No longer a teacher monologue – involving EFL writing learners in teachers' assessment and feedback processes. *Taiwan Journal of TESOL*, *13*(1), 1-31. http://www.tjtesol.org/attachments/article/402/04_TJTESOL-273.pdf

This peer-reviewed article presents a learning-oriented FA design in EFL writing courses at a university in northern Taiwan. The main purpose was to show students' gradual improvement with FA implementations based on repetitions on assessing and reflecting. Four revised and assessed drafts of essays with comments and scores were integrated. These essays were followed up by discussions. Individuals' interviews were used and teachers-students discussions were used as data for analysis. The results indicated students' gradual progression on writing drafts. The statistical analysis of the four batches of essays showed that learners' work improved and the dialogues prepared them to be more independent learners. This research indicates the importance of FA processes in creating independent critical learners.

Fakeye, D. O. (2016). Secondary school teachers' and students' attitudes towards formative assessment and corrective feedback in English language in Ibadan Metropolis. *Journal of Educational and Social Research, 6*(2), 141-148. https://doi.org/10.5901/jesr.2016.v6n2p141

This double-blind peer-reviewed article presents the results of a survey that investigated how teachers and students perceived FA and corrective feedback in learning English in a Nigerian context. Descriptive research design of survey was used with 420 secondary students and six teachers in Nigeria. The data analysis instruments that were used were frequency descriptive and t-test statistics. The findings illustrated that students and teachers perceived FA and corrective feedback positively. Moreover, the findings revealed that students should be exposed more to FA practices and teachers should participate in seminars, conferences, and workshops to inform themselves more on the potentials of FA practices. This source, as many other sources of this AB, illustrates the necessity of student engagement in FA practices and teacher training in FA strategies.

Phung, H. V. (2016). Portfolio assessment in second/foreign language pedagogy. *Hawaii Pacific University TESOL Working Paper Series 14*, 90-107. https://www.hpu.edu/research-publications/tesol-working-papers/2016/07HuyPhung.pdf

This refereed article describes the use of portfolio in L2/FL learning as an alternative type of assessment. It critically reviews the literature in relation to portfolios in LL; the review reveals that most use of portfolios have been related to writing. The author offers suggestions for integrating portfolios in LL, supporting the use of technologies. It also highlights the most important benefits and drawbacks of a portfolio. Authenticity and washback are referred to as the most common benefits whereas practicality and reliability are referred to as their main drawbacks. The article also presents an e-portfolio that was implemented in a project-based English course in a university of Vietnam. Both formative and summative assessment were used in this project. The portfolio was chosen as a form of FA suitable to this project as it provided important evidence of authentic artefacts of students' works. This research complements others in this AB that support portfolio as a FA tool and can be useful to those interested in its use as an FA assessment tool in LL.

Seyyedrezaie, Z. S., Ghansoli, B., Shahriari, H., & Fatemi, A. H. (2016). Examining the effects of Google docs-based instruction and peer feedback types (implicit vs. explicit) on EFL learners' writing performance. *CALL-EJ, 17*(1), 35-51. http://callej.org/journal/17-1/Seyyedrezaie_Ghonsooly_Shahriari_Fatemi2016.pdf

This refereed article examines the effects of Google Docs-based instruction and peer feedback types on EFL learners' writing performances. The participants were 96 undergraduate Iranian male and female EFL students. The participants were assigned in two groups: 48 of them were assigned in the Google Docs based group through blended writing instructions, and the other 48 were assigned into the face-to-face writing instruction. Afterwards, each group was divided into two subgroups, one receiving implicit feedback and the other receiving explicit feedback. A quantitative method with an analysis of two-way ANOVA was used. The findings showed that the students who received explicit feedback had better performance than those who received implicit feedback. Moreover, results indicated that Google Docs writing instructions increased students' confidence in their writing performance. This research describes the contribution of technology, in this case, Google Docs, as an FA LL tool.

Shore, J. R., Wolf, M. K., & Heritage, M. (2016). A case study of formative assessment to support teaching of reading comprehension for English learners. *Journal of Educational Research & Innovation, 5*(2), 1-19. https://digscholarship.unco.edu/jeri/vol5/iss2/4

This peer-reviewed article is about a case study from the US which describes the design, development, and piloting of the ELFA system to support EL reading comprehension in the middle grades. This programme was used on a small scale by eight middle urban school teachers. The main target was to investigate whether the ELFA system could be useful for FA. A literature review on FA precedes the overview of the ELFA system. Interviews were used before and after the ELFA. The results indicated that many teachers found the ELFA useful, stating that it corresponded better to their instructional planning than using tests. However, the limitations of this study were the short period and the small sample of teachers and students. The importance of the ELFA system was indicated in other publications in this AB, therefore this research adds further insights in this area.

Tang, L. (2016). Formative assessment in oral English classroom and alleviation of speaking apprehension. *Theory and Practice in Language Studies, 6*(4), 751-756. https://doi.org/10.17507/tpls.0604.12

This peer-reviewed article presents a study that highlights the usefulness of FA practices in reducing Chinese English students' speaking anxiety in oral English classrooms. The data were collected from 155 students (103 females, 52 males) of first-year non-English at West China Normal University. Quantitative (two questionnaires and a pre-test and a post-test) and qualitative (an interview) research tools were utilised to identify the importance of FA practices in oral English classrooms. The findings revealed that FA in the form of self-assessment, peer assessment, and teacher assessment were engaging and effective and reduced students' speaking anxiety. The value of this study lies in the insights it provides in the role FA can play in reducing students' anxiety and stress, particularly when it comes to speaking.

Pinto-Llorente, A. M., Sánchez-Gómez, M. C., García-Peñalvo, F. J., & Martín, S. C. (2016, November). The use of online quizzes for continuous assessment and self-assessment of second-language learners. In *Proceedings of the Fourth International Conference on Technological Ecosystems for Enhancing Multiculturality* (pp. 819-824). https://doi.org/10.1145/3012430.3012612

> This conference proceedings paper from Spain examines the participants' perceptions in practising online assessment and self-assessment quizzes for learning English. The authors describe self-assessment as a process of FA. The research was based on quantitative research and an ex-post facto design. The sample consisted of 358 students aged from 20 to 58. They studied in the Faculty of Education at the Pontifical University of Salamanca, in Spain. The results indicated that students found the use of online quizzes effective and their level of English was improved especially in reading, listening comprehension, grammatical competence, and vocabulary. The value of this study is based on its large number of participants which is something that provides more valid and reliable data about the importance of integrating online quizzes.

Tsagari, D. (2016). Assessment orientations of state primary EFL teachers in two Mediterranean countries. *Center for Educational Policy Studies Journal, 6*(1), 9-30. https://doi.org/10.26529/cepsj.102

> This peer-reviewed article presents a comparative study for the CBLA practices and abilities of Greek and Cypriot EFL primary teachers. The author highlights the importance of classroom-based assessment

knowledge that teachers should have in order to increase students' performance. Moreover, the author states that teachers are not aware of how to implement classroom-based assessment effectively to a great extent, and they do not yet have a clear picture of CBLA practices. The data were collected through mixed-method research with interviews, and an open-ended pre-test questionnaire. The participants were four teachers from Cyprus and four teachers from Greece. The teachers' responses showed that they preferred test-based assessment as they believed it gives a clearer picture of students' performances. According to the author, assessment *for* learning, based on the CEFR for assessment purposes, is very slow in classrooms in Europe, and LL still relies on summative testing of vocabulary, grammar, and writing in the so-called communicative language classroom. The results indicated the need for a clearer idea about the purposes and implementation of FA and for professional training in language assessment. These results support similar earlier findings.

Williamson, K., & Sadera, E. (2016). Electronic formative feedback and its effect on the writing skills of Asian L2 postgraduate students. *DEANZ2016: Conference Proceedings* (pp. 208-210). https://kiwibelma.files.wordpress.com/2016/05/deanz16-conference-proceedings11-april.pdf

This conference proceedings' paper presents the benefits of using online formative feedback for English as an L2 purpose to Asian postgraduate students in improving their writing skills. A PGT Master's programme was implemented at Auckland's Business School, in New Zealand. By integrating this English language programme, the aim was to improve students' L2 academic writing skills. By using electronic formative feedback, students were expected to achieve better results in summative assessment tasks. eGrammarly and Turnitin Quickmark were used. Some considerations of using the software mentioned were related to some complex problems that students faced. One of the problems that was mentioned was that students had to login to Turnitin many times. In general, it seemed students benefited from using electronic formative feedback and improved their writing skills. The authors suggested that this model could be applied by teachers both in online and offline contexts. This research confirms the benefits of integrating technology for FA LL purposes.

Bayat, A., Jamshidipour, A., & Hashemi, M. (2017). The beneficial impacts of applying formative assessment on Iranian university students' anxiety reduction and listening efficacy. *International Journal of Languages' Education and Teaching, 5*(2), 1-11. https://doi.org/10.18298/ijlet.1740

This peer-reviewed article presents a study that examines the positive effects of FA applications on EFL learners' anxiety and listening skills in an Iranian university. The participants were 60 Iranian EFL students aged 19-25 years old. They were separated into an experimental group (30 students) and a control group (30 students). The data collection tools involved a pre-and a post-test. A t-test was used to evaluate the data. The findings showed that formative quizzes provided students with the opportunity to have better results on tests; it reduced their anxiety and improved their listening efficacy. This article confirms other Iranian researchers' findings which support the need to implement more FA than SA practices in Iran.

Caruso, M., Gadd Colombi, A., & Tebbit, S. (2017). Teaching how to listen. Blended learning for the development and assessment of listening skills in a second language. *Journal of University Teaching & Learning Practice, 14*(1), 14. https://files.eric.ed.gov/fulltext/EJ1142367.pdf

This peer-reviewed article presents a blended environment for the assessment of listening skills in an L2. For the purpose of this project, online quizzes were created for two Italian courses at the University of Western Australia. The listening comprehension online quizzes were developed for FA and SA purposes. The research was based on quantitative research and used an anonymous survey as a research tool. The survey was designed with Qualtrics (https://www.qualtrics.com)

with 23 multiple-choice questions. One hundred and ninety-nine (199) students constituted the research sample. Results showed that students perceived online assessment positively and online quizzes improved their listening skills. This source provides useful insights into the assessment of a specific language skill, that of listening. It also contributes to the knowledge and research on the use of technologies in assessment.

Chen, D., & Zhang, L. (2017). Formative assessment of academic English writing for Chinese EFL learners. *TESOL International Journal, 12*(2), 47-64. https://files.eric.ed.gov/fulltext/EJ1247811.pdf

This double-blind peer-reviewed article investigates implementations of FA of AEW of Chinese EFL Learners. The authors connect FA with the constructivism theory of learning. They argue that in constructivism, knowledge is acquired through interaction, and the learner is the centre of assessment and that it can only be achieved in FA settings with self-assessment and peer assessment activities. In that way, learners construct new knowledge and they actively participate in the assessment process. The participants were divided into an experimental (30) and a control group (28). The experimental group received FA and the control group received SA. The data were collected through a mixed-method approach. Quantitative research tools were used like pre- and post-tests of their writings and qualitative research tools like observations and interviews. The findings showed that participants in the experimental group had better outcomes than participants in the control group. Also, learners perceived positively the use of feedback from their peers and their teachers. The contribution of this study is that it gives insights into the theoretical background of FA.

Demirci, C., & Düzenli, H. (2017). Formative value of an active learning strategy: technology-based think-pair-share in an EFL writing classroom. *World Journal of Education, 7*(6), 63-74. https://doi.org/10.5430/wje.v7n6p63

This peer-reviewed article aimed to determine the formative value of the TPS activities in EFL writing classrooms by looking at students' work and to evaluate the effectiveness of such technology-based implementation of the TPS activities based on students' opinions. It explores how a teacher can employ TPS to both promote active learning and conduct FA in a time-efficient way. The TPS includes revision, practices, and reproduction of prior knowledge. TPS activities were designed in Google Docs. The participants were 18 intermediate English university students in an English preparatory programme in Turkey. The researchers employed an exploratory case study. An online questionnaire was provided to learners to express their attitudes towards TPS. Most of the students expressed the feeling that they would like to have similar experiences in the future. The researchers concluded that such TPS activities could serve as FA alternatives for teachers of other disciplines as well. This is another research example that contributed to the knowledge of the use of technology for FA LL purposes.

Naghdipour, B. (2017). Incorporating formative assessment in Iranian EFL writing: a case study. *The Curriculum Journal, 28*(2), 283-299. https://doi.org/10.1080/09585176.2016.1206479

This peer-reviewed article presents a study on how FA can be implemented in EFL for writing purposes. According to the author, there was little evidence of studies that investigated the use of FA for EFL to undergraduate university students. The participants were 34 first-year undergraduate English translation students (27 female and seven male) from an Iranian university. The data were collected through qualitative and quantitative methods. The data collection tools included pre- and post-writing tasks, pre- and post-questionnaires, and semi-structured interviews. A paired samples t-test was conducted to compare the mean scores of their writings between pre- and post-study writing study. The author concluded that teachers should renew their assessment practices in order to meet their students' needs. Also, students confirmed they had positive experiences of FA for language writing. This publication reinforces other Iranian researchers who support the need for further implementation of FA practices in Iran.

Papadima-Sophocleous, S. (2017). L2 assessment and testing teacher education: an exploration of alternative assessment approaches using new technologies. In K. Borthwick, L. Bradley & S. Thouësny (Eds), *CALL in a climate of change: adapting to turbulent global conditions – short papers from EUROCALL 2017* (pp. 248-253). Research-publishing.net. https://doi.org/10.14705/rpnet.2017.eurocall2017.721

> This peer-reviewed short paper is an action research study. It investigates the experiences of L2 practitioners in a module of an MA in CALL that focuses on classroom FA and CALAT education. The whole philosophy of this module, offered by the Cyprus University of Cyprus, was based on constructivist and post-communicative theory of learning. The module lasted 13 weeks in the autumn of 2016. The participants were 12 language practising teachers from different teaching areas (primary and secondary) and different countries. Qualitative and quantitative methods were used and data were collected through questionnaires, reflective journals, and online webinars. The participants had the opportunity not only to learn about the history of language assessment and testing, but also to create their own assessment tasks using technology applications. Moreover, they experienced the idea of FA through the tasks that they were assigned during the module. The findings of this short paper demonstrated that the participants gained knowledge and experience of tools and techniques used for FA purposes such as peer feedback, instructor feedback, portfolios, artefacts, reflective journals, rubrics, and 'can-do lists'. Also, the researcher suggested that more research should be conducted on language assessment and more specifically on FA practices. The value of this study lies in the fact that the number of studies dedicated at MA level that deal with FA hands on experience and teacher education is limited, according to this AB.

Ranalli, J., Link, S., & Chukharev-Hudilainen, E. (2017). Automated writing evaluation for formative assessment of second language writing: investigating the accuracy and usefulness of feedback as part of argument-based validation. *Educational Psychology, 37*(1), 8-25. https://doi.org/10.1080/01443410.2015.1 136407

> This peer-reviewed article investigates the use of AWE and Criterion at a college-level English at an L2 (ESL) writing course. The participants were 82 volunteer students in a US context. The research focused on two inferences: the utilisation one which involved the assumption that Criterion feedback was useful for students to make accurate feedback and the utilisation one which involved the assumption that Criterion feedback is useful for students to make decisions about revision. This research showed that Criterion feedback offered accurate feedback to students and was found useful for students to make decisions about revisions. Moreover, the findings showed that students used Criterion to correct written errors. Although the authors suggested that the findings raised issues such as the validation of formative applications of AWE, they hoped that the study may have helped in identifying the need for greater accountability from the supporters of the use of AWE tools for FA purposes.

Saito, H., & Inoi, S. I. (2017). Junior and senior high school EFL teachers' use of formative assessment: a mixed-methods study. *Language Assessment Quarterly, 14*(3), 213-233. https://doi.org/10.1080/15434303.2017.1351975

> This peer-reviewed article is a mixed-method study conducted in Japan. The study examined the differences of teachers' FA use between junior and senior high school EFL teachers. Wiliam's model of FA strategies was used to examine whether the teachers used FA differently and if so, to examine the factors contributing to these differences. Rubrics, peer assessment, and teacher's observation and feedback were used for formative purposes. The participants in the survey were 727 students; they were divided into three levels of high, middle, and low level of FA use. A quantitative analysis was used with an explanatory sequential mixed-method design. A qualitative method also followed

with interviews and observations. The findings showed that teachers differed in their use of FA and that they used FA in varying degrees. Several theoretical and practical implications also emerged, such as the importance of teacher training, the theoretical contribution of the study, individual differences in FA use, the use of a mixed-methods approach, and the division between FA and SA.

Saliu Abdulahi, D. (2017). Scaffolding writing development: how formative is the feedback? *Moderna språk, 111*(1), 127-155. https://www.duo.uio.no/handle/10852/59613

This peer-reviewed article discusses the students' perceptions of formative feedback practices used in writing lessons, and also to what extent their feedback practices in writing are in line with FA pedagogy. A qualitative method was applied. The participants were 39 first-year upper secondary students from six secondary schools in Norway. The data were collected through observations, combined with FG interviews. The observations took place in English writing classes. The findings showed that students appreciated feedback but they preferred oral feedback through one-to-one discussions with their teachers compared to written feedback. It was suggested not to give graded texts and ask students to reproduce their writings based on teacher's feedback. The findings also revealed an absence of systematic opportunities and requirements for comprehensive work with feedback and revealed that their feedback practices diverge from central FA principles. The study contributes to other existing research publications which indicate that there is no one approach to feedback that could suit everyone.

Saliu Abdulahi, D., Hellekjær, G. O., & Hertzberg, F. (2017). Teachers' (formative) feedback practices in EFL writing classes in Norway. *Journal of Response to Writing, 3*(1), 31-55. https://journalrw.org/index.php/jrw/article/view/69

This peer-reviewed article aims to identify teachers' formative feedback practices in EFL writing classes in Norway. The participants were ten EFL upper secondary school teachers of writing classes from Oslo. A qualitative method was used and data were collected through observations and semi-structured interviews. The findings indicated that, although teachers acknowledge the national curriculum requirements for FA and FA feedback, most of them tend to practise SA feedback practices. This source, as many other sources in this AB, reinforces the findings which reveal the tendency of teachers to recognise the benefits of FA but at the same time their tendency to lean more towards SA practices.

Vågen, M. T. (2017). *Formative assessment in EFL writing: a case study of pupils' perceptions of their feedback practice and attitudes to receiving and using feedback.* Master's thesis. University of Bergen.

This master's thesis is a case study from Norway (Universitas Bergensis); it investigates pupils' experiences and perspectives of FA in EFL writing at secondary school level, and more precisely formative feedback. A qualitative method was used through face-to-face interviews with pupils. The participants were eight pupils from two tenth grade English classes of a lower secondary school in Norway. The findings showed that pupils preferred precise comments with accompanied examples. The majority of the pupils believed their writing skills had improved due to feedback; however, they had different experiences, therefore different attitudes to its impact on their text writing skills. They also indicate students are positive about the practice of revisiting texts for feedback. Findings also confirmed that students use different strategies to process and take advantage of the information provided through feedback. However, the majority acknowledged the importance of feedback. This study also underlines the importance of providing precise and on-time feedback to students.

Wang, X. (2017). A Chinese EFL teacher's classroom assessment practices. *Language Assessment Quarterly, 14*(4), 312-327. https://doi.org/10.1080/15434303.2017.1393819

This peer-reviewed article is a case study from China. It presents the simultaneous experiences of FA and SA practices from an EFL teacher in China. The author states that Chinese EFL teachers have difficulty in putting FA theories in action and their assessment practices are dominated by SA with tests and exams. For that reason, an experienced EFL teacher was chosen from an FL university in China to participate in this study. The EFL teacher had to provide suggestions to EFL teachers by assessing her students in an oral English course. The participants were 25 first-year English major undergraduates in an EFL public speaking course. The data were collected over one semester. Data collection tools included a teacher's interview, a students' questionnaire, lessons' observations, students' journals, and interviews. The findings indicated that there should be an alignment between the curriculum objectives, classroom instruction, and student assessment. Also, it was found out that the use of FA and SA practices can encourage students to increase their learning goals. This article is an example of classroom assessment being conducted through both formative and SA, with some assessment practices serving practices of both FA and SA. This was implemented in a productive way that aimed to help students make progress in an upward spiral. The article concludes with the importance of bridging the gap between assessment theories and classroom practices by bringing experienced teachers' classroom assessment expertise to the attention of other teachers.

Widiastuti, I. A. M. S., & Saukah, A. (2017). Formative assessment in EFL classroom practices. *Bahasa dan Seni: Jurnal Bahasa, Sastra, Seni, dan Pengajarannya, 45*(1), 50-63. https://doi.org/10.17977/um015v45i12017p050

This reviewed article aimed to explore challenges and opportunities of FA implementations in EFL classrooms in Indonesia. Qualitative method was implemented to collect data through semi-structured interviews with three English junior high school teachers and three students. The aim was to find out about the English teachers' understanding of FA and the follow up actions taken by them after the implementation of FA.

The findings revealed that the teachers needed a better understanding of FA in order to follow appropriate action strategies, and improve the learning and teaching processes for better student learning achievement. This study substantiates what others have already supported about the fact that teachers still need a further and deeper understanding of FA characteristics and practices.

Saglam, A. L. G. (2018). The integration of educational technology for classroom-based formative assessment to empower teaching and learning. In A. Khan & S. Umair (Eds), *Handbook of research on mobile devices and smart gadgets in K-12 rducation* (pp. 321-341). IGI Global. https://doi.org/10.4018/978-1-5225-2706-0.ch020

This reviewed handbook chapter from Turkey discusses the importance of Web 2.0 tools in CBLA; it provides a descriptive list of tools such as Socrative, Nearpod, and Quizegg which can be used as FA LL tools. The author claims that FA is a reflective procedure for the teacher about how the lesson is going on and learners can benefit from ongoing feedback. The author suggested that teachers should be encouraged to explore the integration of Web 2.0 tools for FA purposes. This publication shows how Web 2.0 tools can enhance FA LL.

Guadu, Z. B., & Boersma, E. J. (2018). EFL instructors' beliefs and practices of formative assessment in teaching writing. *Journal of Language Teaching and Research*, *9*(1), 42-50. https://doi.org/10.17507/jltr.0901.06

This peer-reviewed article presents a mixed-method study, which seeks to investigate EFL instructors' beliefs and practices of FA in teaching writing, and to determine the relationship between their beliefs and practices of FA in an Ethiopian context. The data were collected through qualitative and quantitative methods. The participants were 27 Debre Makos university EFL instructors. Qualitative data were collected through a questionnaire, semi-structured interviews, and students' marked paragraphs and essay papers. Quantitative data were analysed through descriptive and inferential statistics (correlation). Although the findings showed that the instructors believed FA was important in maximising instruction and student learning, they also revealed limitations on instructors' practice of FA. This source highlights some factors as setbacks in the assessment process. These included time constraints, large and unmanageable class sizes, and students' illegible hand-writing.

Joyce, P. (2018). The effectiveness of online and paper-based formative assessment in the Learning of English as a second language. *PASAA, 5,* 126-146. https://www.culi.chula.ac.th/publicationsonline/files/article/W8Mo0m4nyBMon110741.pdf

This peer-reviewed study compares online and paper-based FA in ESL. The participants were 145 L2 Japanese University students. Seventy-four of them took online quizzes, while 71 were given paper-based quizzes. Both groups had quizzes for homework as FA. The study lasted for 15 weeks. The online homework group received their FA through Moodle. The students took 31 multiple-choice online quizzes. Both classes had the same teacher and followed the same syllabus. Also, both groups had a summative assessment at the end of the course by taking the TOEIC test. Correlation and regression analysis were used to compare the data from the two groups. The results indicated a significant relationship between the online FA and summative exam scores, unlike in the case of the paper-based FA. The findings also revealed the contribution of the use of technologies: according to the author, the effectiveness of the online formative quizzes was influenced by factors such as the immediacy of feedback, the opportunity and incentive to resubmit quizzes, and quiz functionality. This research contributes further to the use of technologies in FA LL.

Lam, R. (2018). Understanding assessment as learning in writing classrooms: the case of portfolio assessment. *Iranian Journal of Language Teaching Research, 6*(3), 19-36. https://doi.org/10.30466/ijltr.2018.120599

This peer-reviewed article from Hong Kong presents AAS and its relation to writing assessment and suggests ways to include it into existing curriculum and policy. The article is separated into five sections. The first section presents the definition, principles and purposes of AaL. The second part discusses the theoretical background of AaL and its underpinnings using the theories of FA and self-regulated learning, focusing on internal feedback in learning and its relation to writing assessment. The third section describes writing assessment trends; the fourth part describes the case of the adoption of a portfolio as a tool for assessing writing and putting AaL into practice. It reports that AaL can be considered as a subset of FA and its main aim is to support learning with reflection. This article contributes to the formation of a theoretical lens of AAL (FA and self-regulated learning), provides new insights into AaL in practice through the description of a case of writing portfolio assessment and raises some concern in the application of AaL in the regional and international writing classroom context.

Meissner, M. C. (2018). *Formative assessment at the intersection of principles, practice and perceptions*. Master's thesis. Faculty of Education and Natural Sciences, Inland Norway University of Applied Sciences. https://brage.inn.no/inn-xmlui/bitstream/handle/11250/2560247/Meissner.pdf?sequence=1

This Master's thesis examines FA of writing in the English subject in Norway, focusing on formative feedback. The possible challenges of FA were explored. The feedback of seven teachers to a student text, and their thoughts on why they chose to comment the way they did, as well as students' perceptions of feedback practices and preferences were examined. The teachers indicated the importance of context in FA. The results also indicated that students found that quality, amount, and timing of feedback have an impact. Although motivated by feedback, students are still influenced by summative assessment and preferred formative feedback in conjunction with grades. This entry gives insights into research in the area of FA of writing in English. It is also an example of research conducted at the doctorate level.

Ponce, H. R., Mayer, R. E., Figueroa, V. A., & López, M. J. (2018). Interactive highlighting for just-in-time formative assessment during whole-class instruction: effects on vocabulary learning and reading comprehension. *Interactive Learning Environments, 26*(1), 42-60. https://doi.org/10.1080/10494820.2017.1282878

> This peer-reviewed article describes the use of a software for FA purposes by implementing an interactive highlighting vocabulary method. FA was used to establish students' knowledge in order to use the information to adapt the lesson. The research was conducted in Chile. Students were given a passage and they highlighted their unknown words. These words were shown on their instructor's screen: in red the words most highlighted, in orange the second most highlighted and in yellow the third most highlighted. The instructor then created some activities based on students' unknown words. The findings from experimental studies to college and high school students in a ten-week programme revealed that students who interactively highlighted their unknown words outperformed in vocabulary tests to other groups that studied without interactive highlighting. This research maintains that interactive highlighting can be used as an important FA tool. It adds to the research topics of FA in LL.

Sardareh, S. (2018). Formative feedback in a Malaysian primary school ESL context. *MOJES: Malaysian Online Journal of Educational Sciences, 4*(1), 1-8. https://mojes.um.edu.my/article/view/12640

> This double-blind peer-reviewed article investigates the FA applications in primary school in Malaysia and its ESL context, in times during when FA was introduced as part of new transformations by the Malaysian Ministry of Education. Although the article focuses on FA, it does not dedicate any section in what FA entails, which would have clearly indicated the author's background knowledge of the notion of FA. Qualitative method was used in the form of classroom observations and FG discussions of English language teachers. Three ESL teachers from different Malaysian schools participated in this project. The findings

> showed that teachers did not use feedback effectively. They used feedback as a means of praise and not as a means of indicating students where they stand. The findings also revealed that teachers did not have knowledge in providing effective feedback. This study confirms the findings of others which emphasise on the necessity of teacher training on FA strategies in LL.

Stabler-Havener, M. L. (2018). Defining, conceptualising, problematising, and assessing language teacher assessment literacy. *Studies in Applied Linguistics and TESOL, 18*(1). https://doi.org/10.7916/salt.v18i1.1195

> This peer-reviewed article reviews the literature on language teacher LAL. It explores LAL definitions and conceptualisations. It also investigates pre- and in-service teacher education and resources used in LAL teacher development, and examines the ways teachers' LAL levels are assessed. The discussion of the article language teacher LAL included FA: teacher knowledge of FA, FA practices, and inclusion of FA in teacher education. The article concludes that it is difficult to generalise how LAL should be defined, conceptualised, problematised, and assessed. The source provides useful information on LAL and FA within the LAL framework.

Tavakoli, E., Amirian, S. M. R., Burner, T., Davoudi, M., & Ghaniabadi, S. (2018). Operationalization of formative assessment in writing: an intuitive approach to the development of an instrument. *Applied Research on English Language, 7*(3), 319-344. https://doi.org/10.22108/ARE.2018.112373.1340

> This peer-reviewed article shares the processes of the design of a FAoW instrument, which was based on a feedback model of Black and Wiliam's (2009) and Hattie and Timperley's (2007) FA. The FAoW instrument was developed as part of a PhD project in Iran. Following a comprehensive literature review, an instrument was designed. Its aim was to measure students' experiences of FA practices and their attitudes towards them in EFL writing classrooms. The design of FAoW

was based on three phases of writing feedback: where the learner is going/pre-writing, where the learner is right now/writing, and how to get there post-writing. Experts in a focused group classified the instrument items according to five FA components. The outcomes were item revisions and additions, and the experts agreed that the FAoW instrument reflected the theoretical frameworks of FA. This entry can prove useful to those who are interested in developing such instruments or using this instrument in other contexts.

Alam, M. (2019). Assessment challenges & impact of formative portfolio assessment (FPA) on EFL learners' writing performance: a case study on the preparatory English language course. *English Language Teaching, 12*(7), 161-172. https://doi.org/10.5539/elt.v12n7p161

The present peer-reviewed pilot study originating from Saudi Arabia investigates the role of portfolio assessment on EFL learners in writing skills. The participants were 40 (20 male and 20 female) undergraduate EFL university students. They were divided into a control and an experimental group. An experiment research design was applied. Pre-tests and post-tests were given to both groups. Also, writing tests and interviews were used. The experiment group was introduced to the use of portfolio for FA purposes, whereas the control group experienced only traditional assessment. The results indicated that the use of portfolio for FA purposes had a positive impact on students' writing performance and it was estimated that the level of students' anxiety was lower. The value of this research lies in the fact that it gives insights, as other publications in this AB, to the role of portfolios as an FA tool for EFL learning. Moreover, at the end, the author provides some useful recommendations for teachers on PA implementation.

Alzaid, F., & Alkarzae, N. (2019). *The effects of paper, web, and game based formative assessment on motivation and learning: a literature review.* https://files.eric.ed.gov/fulltext/ED594189.pdf

This literature review from Saudi Arabia compares three methods of FA; paper-based, web-based, and game based. It is stated that in many educational systems, FA is misused in ESL and EFL learning. Also, it informs that paper-based FA is produced by pencil and paper quizzes. Technology-based FA provides opportunities to the learner to try to achieve a task many times and receive instant feedback in comparison to paper-based assessment. A reward system learning, with the use of badges, leaderboards, and immediate feedback is presented. Furthermore, the authors conclude that web-based assessments offer more opportunities for FA than paper-based and improve the learners' motivation and level of memory. In the end, the authors suggest the necessity for further research of gamification's role in FA. This article shows examples of misusing FA worldwide, specifically in Hong Kong where there is a dominance of the high stakes examination system. Students usually receive grades with feedback that informs them of their progress rather than receiving qualitative feedback during the process of writing. FA, as the authors argue, should be used as a learning-oriented process with the provision of ongoing structured feedback. This is an approach that many educational systems worldwide could adopt.

Can Daşkın, N., & Hatipoğlu, Ç. (2019). Reference to a past learning event as a practice of informal formative assessment in L2 classroom interaction. *Language Testing, 36*(4), 527-551. https://doi.org/10.1177/0265532219857066

This peer-reviewed article investigates the role of informal FA in a preparatory school of a state university in Turkey. The term informal FA is used to refer to FA practices that are related to everyday learning activities. In an informal FA setting, the teacher responds quickly, spontaneously, and flexibly in the classroom. For this study, a corpus of video recordings of an EFL class (55 classroom hours) was used. The class consisted of 32 students (seven male and 25 female). The research methodology was based on CA which is the study of "recorded, naturally occurring talk in-interaction". Also, the study was based on an RPLE. The RPLE occurs when the teacher focuses on activities or topics that are presented in a past learning event. The findings showed that the RPLE aims to find evidence of student knowledge and to correct previous knowledge from the teacher. According to the authors, this study bridges some of the gap between language assessment and classroom research, supporting that teachers' ability to conduct informal FA is of great importance, therefore it has implications in language teacher education.

Cong-Lem, N. (2019). Portfolios as learning and alternative assessment tools in EFL context: a review. *CALL-EJ. 20*(2), 165-180.

This review from Vietnam reports on the use of portfolios as learning and alternative assessment tools in EFL contexts. It reports on the educational affordances and challenges of portfolio based learning in EFL. It also suggests a framework of portfolio based learning. The review search resulted in 19 research papers that met the set of predefined criteria. The results included the theoretical frameworks for portfolio based learning, the specific stages of its implementation, and its affordances. FA was only briefly addressed in the discussion as one of the themes of the findings. It was argued that the portfolio could be considered as a form of FA, which could promote students' learning.

Cotter, M., & Hinkelman, D. (2019). Video assessment module: self, peer, and teacher post-performance assessment for learning. In F. Meunier, J. Van de Vyver, L. Bradley & S. Thouësny (Eds), *CALL and complexity – short papers from EUROCALL 2019* (pp. 94-99). Research-publishing.net. https://doi.org/10.14705/rpnet.2019.38.992

This peer-reviewed short paper is a report of a ten-year action research study conducted in Japan. It is based on a VAM developed by Sapporo Gakuin University. The participants were 50-60 second-year English major Japanese students. With VAM, teachers could record English presentations and upload them to the module for their students for self and peer assessment. Qualitative and quantitative methods were used. The results indicated that VAM enabled teachers to manage their time better; it also helped students to use the tool asynchronously without being anxious or feeling pressured by time. Moreover, the findings showed the value in using VAM by both teachers and students. It was suggested that student training in the use of online rubrics to score presentations efficiently gave further validity. The authors concluded that the ten-year of action research of post-performance video watching and self and peer assessment proved a successful formative tool.

Davison, C. (2019). Using assessment to enhance learning in English language education. In X. Gao (Ed.), *Second handbook of English language teaching*. Springer International Handbooks of Education. Springer. https://doi.org/10.1007/978-3-030-02899-2_21

The author of this peer-reviewed chapter argues that although the concept of using assessment to enhance learning in teaching in ESL/additional language education has been present in the past ten years, there is still a lack of any consensus about terminology and scope, and enough examples of large-scale assessment systems, where the principles of the concept are reflected in practice. For this reason, the author first explores the definition and scope discussed by many researchers in earlier research (e.g. classroom-based assessment, FA, assessment *for* learning, dynamic assessment, LOA), in order to establish the latest in the area. Then Davison presents an example of a large-scale assessment system, the tools to enhance assessment literacy for TEAL, which exemplifies the core attributes of the concept. This assessment system was based on researchers-teachers' collaborations of EAL specialists in Australia. It was developed following the principles of the Vygotskian theory of learning. The TEAL project was used since mid-2015 as an online assessment tool for more than 40,000 English language teachers in Victorian schools in Australia. It has also attracted the attention of an international audience (more than 10,000 page views per month from over 20 countries). External evaluations found the system, among other things, theoretically and philosophically coherent, and able to model desired outcomes. This research also surfaced some unresolved issues such as the role of the learner and the literacy of the teacher. This work comes to support earlier studies which reported that language teachers still need more support and guidance in language assessment.

Gan, Z., & Leung, C. (2019). Illustrating formative assessment in task-based language teaching. *ELT Journal, 72,* 10-19. https://doi.org/10.1093/ELT/CCZ048

The purpose of this peer-reviewed article from Hong Kong is first to review the most recent discussion on FA in both general education and L2 assessment fields. The article then demonstrated how FA was naturally embedded into a three-stage cycle of task-based ESL classroom grammar teaching and learning activities and improved both learning and assessment practices. The authors conclude that, with the relevant support, guidance, and training, L2 educators can change their summative-oriented practices to more FA ones. This review can be a useful guidance on how FA can be implemented in task-based language teaching in the daily ESL classroom.

Heritage, M. (2019). Feedback for enhanced English language learning. In X. Gao (Ed.), *Second handbook of English language teaching* (pp. 497-515). Springer International Handbooks of Education. Springer. https://doi.org/10.1007/978-3-030-02899-2_27

This chapter from the US presents effective feedback practices, in the context of FA, in language teaching. First it discussed FA as integral to teaching and learning. It distinguishes between FA feedback and feedback as a response to error. The chapter illustrates instances of feedback for LL through video recording transcripts. Moreover, illustrations of formative feedback in communicative content-based teaching and learning are presented. The author concludes by describing the knowledge and skills teachers need to engage in FA and stresses the need for language teacher training in that area. This review can be a useful guidance on how FA and feedback practices can be implemented in language teaching.

Kızıl, V., & Yumru, H. (2019). The impact of self-assessment: a case study on a tertiary level EFL writing class. *Mevzu – Sosyal Bilimler Dergisi, 1*, 35-54. https://dergipark.org.tr/en/pub/mevzu/issue/44858/517475

This peer-reviewed article is a seven-week case study which investigates the benefits of self-assessment as a form of FA in EFL writing lessons at the tertiary level in Turkey, and how self-assessment contributes to metacognition. The participants were 17 students, 12 male and five female university students from an English preparation programme. They engaged in a series of writing tasks. They were required to assess their own writing with the use of rubrics and conduct self-assessment. The data were collected through a pre- and post-questionnaire and analysed with the use of the IBM SPSS Statistics software (Version 25) and a paired sample t-test. The results showed that self-assessment as a form of FA had a positive effect on students' writing skills and the development of their metacognitive skills. This source reinforces the results of earlier research, which supported that self-assessment is an important characteristic of FA.

Şişman, E. P., & Büyükkarci, K. (2019). A review of foreign language teachers' assessment literacy. *Sakarya University Journal of Education, 9*(3), 628-650. https://doi.org/10.19126/suje.621319

This is a peer-reviewed review of the literature for FL/L2 teachers' language assessment from 1987 to 2019. It includes 82 research studies and articles from Turkey, the authors' base, and other countries in the world. The compilation method was used as a research method to review the literature. Some subtopics of this review are international LAL studies and language assessment literacy studies

> on Turkey. The review concludes that language assessment courses were found insufficient and there was an imbalance between theory and practice. Also, most language teachers emphasised standardised tests and it was proved that they lack knowledge in real-life tasks and in implementing FA. Many teachers also expressed the need for training and put more theory into practice. This review gives informative insights into LAL from 1987 to 2019 that could be of valuable assistance to language teachers to this day.

Vassiliou, S., & Papadima-Sophocleous, S. (2019). A systematic review and annotated bibliography of second language learning formative assessment: an overview. *Conference Proceedings, 12th International Conference Innovation in Language Learning* (pp. 352-362). https://conference.pixel-online.net/ICT4LL/files/ict4ll/ed0012/Conference%20Proceedings.pdf

> This peer-reviewed conference procceding's paper from Cyprus gives a summative overview of a SR and a descriptive and evaluative AB of L2FA from 2000 to 2017. The SR included 108 publications. The AB consisted of a series of bibliographical entries and citations. The combination of the SR and the AB aimed to provide a first more rounded overview of L2 FA. The findings provided considerable information to L2 researchers, practitioners, and educators, such as: the role of technology in L2 FA; the dominance of the English language in L2 FA practices; the dominance of L2 FA practices in higher education; and a total of 96.3% reported a positive impact of L2 FA implementations on students' motivation and progress. The study gives suggestions for further research such as the need for teachers' training in L2 FA. This publication can be seen as a step towards a systematic recording of activities in the area of FA in LL.

Tavakoli, E., Amirian, M. R., Burner, T., Davoudi, M., & Ghaniabadi, S. (2019). Formative assessment of writing (FAoW): a confirmatory factor structure study. *International Journal of Assessment Tools in Education, 6*(3), 344-361. https://doi.org/10.21449/ijate.544277

This peer-reviewed validation study aimed to identify EFL learners' experiences of FAoW. A 50 Likert scale item instrument was piloted through interviews with three EFL learners, and administered in a large-scale on a sample of 315 Iranian students from three non-state language schools and five universities for factor structuring and construct validation. A FAoW framework with five FA factor solutions (e.g. clarifying criteria, evidence on students' current learning, feedback to move learners forward, peer assessment, and autonomy) evaluated through a CFA with AMOS 22, and subsequently a FAoW framework with three FA factor solutions (e.g. clarifying criteria, peer assessment, and feedback) in two stages of pre- and while-writing revealed that, in the view of EFL students, FAoW was found to be practised within its full potential with the three components. The findings of this study provided a set of FAoW practices suggesting an ideal FAoW model for EFL contexts, and complemented earlier studies. This instrument has the potential to be utilised by other researchers in other contexts and writing classrooms.

Xie, Q., & Lei, Y. (2019). Formative assessment in primary English writing classes: a case study from Hong Kong. *The Asian EFL Journal, 23*(5), 55-95.

In this peer-reviewed case study from Hong Kong, there were three participating teachers: a novice, an experienced, and a veteran. Their instructional, assessment, and feedback practices throughout the pre-, during-, and post-stages of an L2 writing instruction cycle were examined. A widely cited framework of FA strategies was adopted for this examination. The data were collected through interviews, lesson observations, teaching materials, students' writing, and teacher written feedback. The results showed that all teachers were more engaged with the pre-writing and post-writing phase and not with the during-writing phase. Also, effective feedback, as stated in this research, is related to the process pedagogy and the multiple drafting. This source reports the importance of feedback as a key component of FA. It also proposes a checklist that integrates effective instructional strategies with FA strategies and suggests their application at different stages of the language writing instruction process. Its findings can be useful to other researchers and constitutes an addition to the current literature.

Alharbi, A. S., & Meccawy, Z. (2020). Introducing Socrative as a tool for formative assessment in Saudi EFL classrooms. *Arab World English Journal*, *11*(3), 372-384.

This study explored Saudi EFL university learners' attitudes towards the use of mobile-based tests as a form of classroom FA and investigated the effect of their first experience of *Socrative* as a tool of FA on their attitudes towards the use of mobile-based testing. Participants were 35 female students that were enrolled in an ESP at a state university in Saudi Arabia. *Socrative* is a web-based platform that can be accessed using any browser. The study followed a pre- and post-experiment design. Participants responded to pre- experiment surveys towards their attitudes on the use of mobile phones in their language assessment and a post-experiment survey about their perspectives and experiences after using *Socrative*. The experiment included three tools: a pre-experiment survey, a *Socrative* quiz, and a post-experiment survey. Results revealed that there was a significant difference among learners before and after the use of mobile-based tests. This was attributed to the use of *Socrative* quiz as an assessment tool, and its features (e.g. instant feedback, picture clues, answer explanation, and total score display), that are not found in the traditional paper-based tests. After the use, learners found *Socrative* as a positive encouraging and supporting tool for language assessment. The results are in line with earlier similar studies. This source also makes reference to the recent COVID-19 pandemic experience, which transformed many educational practices and drew attention to the potentials of technology in education in general and in LL and assessment in particular. The information at hand is important for future practices of FA, especially due to the changes caused by the crisis of the Covid-19 pandemic.

Al-Mofti, K. W. H. (2020). Challenges of implementing formative assessment: by Iraqi EFL instructors at university level. *Koya University Journal of Humanities and Social Sciences*, *3*(1), 181-189.

>This peer-reviewed article investigates the implementations of FA strategies in an Iraqi university and the challenges that EFL instructors faced. The author states that in Iraq there is a tendency towards SA and there is a lack of FA explorations in EFL teaching. Therefore, another aim of this study was to fill in this gap, since there was no other research conducted in Iraq showing the challenges that EFL instructors are dealing with FA use in EFL context. The researcher used mainly qualitative research methods to obtain data. Semi-structured interviews with three different EFL teachers and observations from six different classes from the three Iraqi different universities were used. Quantitative analysis also was used only in a few instances to count the frequency of FA that EFL Iraqi teachers used and its' challenges' implementations. From the instructors' interviews and lessons' observations many challenges were revealed, such as instructors' inexperience to create assessment criteria, and students' inability to provide feedback to themselves and their peers. Also, worth mentioning is the fact that many instructors claimed that peer-assessing creates tensions among students because they "do not perceive the value of assessment as part of learning but rather as judgement". Many instructors also agreed that FA strategies are time-consuming for them, especially the creation of quizzes to check students' understanding. They reported as well that for them it is a priority to finish the curriculum and then conduct any FA use. The author suggested that EFL Iraqi instructors needed training on how to use FA effectively in the future. This source illustrates some important issues related to FA implementations. FA should be considered as an integral part of the curriculum and not be seen as a separate concept. EFL instructors should be given more training opportunities in FA use in order to cater for any misconceptions.

Ammar, A. (2020). *Impact of formative assessment on raising students' motivation: case of third year EFl students at the university of El-Oued.* Doctoral dissertation. University of Tlemcen.

> This PhD dissertation from Algeria discusses the impact of FA on raising EFL university students' motivation. Also, this study aims to explore teachers' practices in enhancing students' perceptions in the FA process. The author describes the FA system which consists of feed-up, feedback, and feed-forward. Feed-up ensures students' understanding of the purpose of the assignment, feedback informs students for their performance, and feed-forward shows where learning should move on. In this PhD dissertation, a literature review is carried out of the concepts of FA, students and teachers' roles in FA, the role of formative feedback, and the role of FA in the development of students' motivation. A descriptive case study was selected as a research design. Two questionnaires and classroom observation were used as research tools. Participants were 100 third year EFL students, 77 females and 23 males, who studied in the Department of English language at El-Oued University during the academic year 2015-2016. Findings showed that FA practices have raised students' performances in the target language and, according to their responses from the questionnaire, they felt more engaged by self-assessing their learning. The results also indicated a good understanding of FA practices by the instructors and that this understanding was enriched during their FA practices. The author also provides some suggestions for further considerations for research, like the effectiveness of technology-enhanced FA tools and the identification of the FA practices that work better for learning a foreign language. A very important conclusion of this dissertation is that the author states that formative feedback should be provided by teachers more frequently, earlier, and positively. This doctorate dissertation is another indication that there is interest in FA practices at the doctorate level.

Widiastuti, I. A. M. S., Mukminatien, N., Prayogo, J. A., & Irawati, E. (2020). Dissonances between teachers' beliefs and practices of formative assessment in EFL classes. *International Journal of Instruction, 13*(1), 71-84. https://doi.org/10.29333/iji.2020.13l5a

> This peer-reviewed article from Indonesia investigates the discrepancy between teachers' beliefs and practices of FA in EFL classes. Multi-case studies were carried out. Participants were three EFL teachers with different levels of CPD participation. A qualitative method was implemented with semi-structured interviews, observation, and document studies. Results showed that although teachers with CPD participation level had stronger beliefs in FA compared to those with lower on, this had no real impact on the success of their FA practices. Factors that were identified as influencing their beliefs were time allocation, teachers' workload, and classroom conditions. Although the small number of participants is a limitation, this study endorsed earlier research that identifies and suggests further exploration of the relation between teachers' beliefs and practices.

Yarahmadzehi, N., & Goodarzi, M. (2020). Investigating the role of formative mobile-based assessment in vocabulary learning of pre-intermediate EFL learners in comparison with paper-based assessment. *Turkish Online Journal of Distance Education, 21*(1), 181-196.

> This peer-reviewed article sought to investigate if there is any significant difference between the vocabulary gain of Iranian pre-intermediate EFL learners assessed formatively by paper and pen and those assessed formatively using a mobile device. It also studied the attitude of Iranian pre-intermediate EFL learners towards mobile-based assessment. Participants were 40 pre-intermediate EFL learners who studied general English language at Chabahar Maritime University of Iran. A quasi-experimental design with a pre-test, treatment and a post-test were used to answer the research question. The group that was assessed formatively used the Socrative mobile application. Learners' vocabulary was formatively assessed during a period of ten sessions. Although there was no statistically significant difference between the

two groups before the treatment, the results after the treatment indicated that the mean score of the students using technology was higher than the students whose assessment was based on pen-and-paper, and that there was a statistically significant difference between the two groups after the treatment. The analysis of both qualitative and quantitative data also revealed that students demonstrated a positive attitude towards mobile-based vocabulary FA. This study raises some important issues that are related to FA implementations: the assessment literacy of language teachers and the benefits of technology affordances in FA practices.

References

Absalom, M., & De Saint Léger, D. (2011). Reflecting on reflection learner perceptions of diaries and blogs in tertiary language study. *Arts and Humanities in Higher Education, 10*(2), 189-211. https://doi.org/10.1177/1474022210389141

Al-Mofti, K. W. H. (2020). Challenges of implementing formative assessment: by Iraqi EFL instructors at university level. *Koya University Journal of Humanities and Social Sciences, 3*(1), 181-189.

Alam, M. (2019). Assessment challenges & impact of formative portfolio assessment (FPA) on EFL learners' writing performance: a case study on the preparatory English language course. *English Language Teaching, 12*(7), 161-172. https://doi.org/10.5539/elt.v12n7p161

Alderson, J. C., & Banerjee, J. (2001). Language testing and assessment (part I). *Language Teaching, 34*(4), 213-236. https://doi.org/10.1017/S0261444800014464

Alharbi, A. S., & Meccawy, Z. (2020). Introducing Socrative as a tool for formative assessment in Saudi EFL classrooms. Arab World English Journal, 11(3), 372-384.

Alvarez, L., Ananda, S., Walqui, A., Sato, E., & Rabinowitz, S. (2014). *Focusing formative assessment on the needs of English language learners*. https://www.wested.org/wp-content/uploads/2016/11/1391626953FormativeAssessment_report5-3.pdf

Alzaid, F., & Alkarzae, N. (2019). *The effects of paper, web, and game based formative assessment on motivation and learning: a literature review*. https://files.eric.ed.gov/fulltext/ED594189.pdf

Ammar, A. (2020). *Impact of formative assessment on raising students' motivation: case of third year EFl students at the university of El-Oued*. Doctoral dissertation. University of Tlemcen.

Babaee, M., & Tikoduadua, M. (2013). E-portfolios: a new trend in formative writing assessment. International Journal of Modern Education Forum (IJMEF), 2(2), 49-56.

Bachelor, J. W., & Bachelor, R. B. (2016). Classroom currency as a means of formative feedback, reflection, and assessment in the world language classroom. *NECTFL Review*, *78*, 31-42. https://files.eric.ed.gov/fulltext/EJ1256488.pdf

Bahati, B., Tedre, M., Fors, U., & Evode, M. (2016). Exploring feedback practises in formative assessment in Rwandan higher education: a multifaceted approach is needed. *International Journal of Teaching and Education*, *4*(2), 1-22. https://doi.org/10.20472/TE.2016.4.2.001

Bayat, A., Jamshidipour, A., & Hashemi, M. (2017). The beneficial impacts of applying formative assessment on Iranian university students' anxiety reduction and listening efficacy. *International Journal of Languages' Education and Teaching*, *5*(2), 1-11. https://doi.org/10.18298/ijlet.1740

Black, P., & Jones, J. (2006). Formative assessment and the learning and teaching of MFL: sharing the language learning road map with the learners. *Language Learning Journal*, *34*(1), 4-9. https://doi.org/10.1080/09571730685200171

Black, P., & Wiliam, D. (1998). Assessment and classroom learning. *Assessment in Education, Principles, Policy & Practice*, *5*(1), 7-74. https://doi.org/10.1080/0969595980050102

Black, P., & Wiliam, D. (2009). Developing the theory of formative assessment. *Educational Assessment, Evaluation and Accountability*, *21*(1), 5-31. https://doi.org/10.1007/s11092-008-9068-5

Boud, D., Cohen, R., & Sampson, J. (1999). Peer learning and assessment. *Assessment and Evaluation in Higher Education*, *24*(4), 413-426. https://doi.org/10.1080/0260293990240405

Burner, T. (2014). The potential formative benefits of portfolio assessment in second and foreign language writing contexts: a review of the literature. *Studies in Educational Evaluation*, *43*, 139-149. https://doi.org/10.1016/j.stueduc.2014.03.002

Burner, T. (2016). Formative assessment of writing in English as a foreign language. *Scandinavian Journal of Educational Research*, *60*(6), 626-648. https://doi.org/10.1080/00313831.2015.1066430

Buttram, C., MacMillan, D., & Koch, Dr. R. T. (2012). *Comparing the annotated bibliography to the literature review.* UNA Center for Writing excellence. https://www.una.edu/writingcenter/docs/Writing-Resources/Comparing%20the%20Annotated%20Bibliography%20to%20the%20Literature%20Review.pdf

Buyukkarci, K. (2010). *The effect of formative assessment on learners' test anxiety and assessment preferences in EFL context.* Unpublished doctoral dissertation. Cukurova University. http://libratez.cu.edu.tr/tezler/8059.pdf

Can Daşkın, N., & Hatipoğlu, Ç. (2019). Reference to a past learning event as a practice of informal formative assessment in L2 classroom interaction. *Language Testing, 36*(4), 527-551. https://doi.org/10.1177/0265532219857066

Carless, D. R. (2002). The mini-viva as a tool to enhance assessment for learning. *Assessment & Evaluation in Higher Education, 27*(4), 353-363. https://doi.org/10.1080/0260293022000001364

Carreira, M. M. (2012). Formative assessment in HL teaching: purposes, procedures, and practices. *Heritage Language Journal, 9*(1), 100-120. https://doi.org/10.46538/hlj.9.1.6

Caruso, M., Gadd Colombi, A., & Tebbit, S. (2017). Teaching how to listen. Blended learning for the development and assessment of listening skills in a second language. *Journal of University Teaching & Learning Practice, 14*(1), 14. https://files.eric.ed.gov/fulltext/EJ1142367.pdf

Chen, D., & Zhang, L. (2017). Formative assessment of academic English writing for Chinese EFL learners. *TESOL International Journal, 12*(2), 47-64. https://files.eric.ed.gov/fulltext/EJ1247811.pdf

Chen, Q., Kettle, M., Klenowski, V., & May, L. (2013). Interpretations of formative assessment in the teaching of English at two Chinese universities: a sociocultural perspective. *Assessment & Evaluation in Higher Education, 38*(7), 831-846. https://doi.org/10.1080/02602938.2012.726963

Chen, Q., May, L., Klenowski, V., & Kettle, M. (2014). The enactment of formative assessment in English language classrooms in two Chinese universities: teacher and student responses. *Assessment in Education: Principles, Policy & Practice, 21*(3), 271-285. https://doi.org/10.1080/0969594X.2013.790308

Cho, S., & Park, C. (2014). The role of scoring in formative assessment of second language writing. *GEMA Online® Journal of Language Studies, 14*(3). https://doi.org/10.17576/GEMA-2014-1403-07

Colby-Kelly, C., & Turner, C. E. (2007). AFL research in the L2 classroom and evidence of usefulness: taking formative assessment to the next level. *Canadian Modern Language Review*, *64*(1), 9-37. https://doi.org/10.3138/cmlr.64.1.009

Cong-Lem, N. (2019). Portfolios as learning and alternative assessment tools in EFL context: a review. *CALL-EJ. 20*(2), 165-180.

Cotter, M., & Hinkelman, D. (2019). Video assessment module: self, peer, and teacher post-performance assessment for learning. In F. Meunier, J. Van de Vyver, L. Bradley & S. Thouësny (Eds), *CALL and complexity – short papers from EUROCALL 2019* (pp. 94-99). Research-publishing.net. https://doi.org/10.14705/rpnet.2019.38.992

Crusan, D., Plakans, L., & Gebril, A. (2016). Writing assessment literacy: surveying second language teachers' knowledge, beliefs, and practices. *Assessing Writing*, *28*, 43-56. https://doi.org/10.1016/j.asw.2016.03.001

Cummins, P. W., & Davesne, C. (2009). Using electronic portfolios for second language assessment. *The Modern Language Journal*, *93*(1), 848-867. https://doi.org/10.1111/j.1540-4781.2009.00977.x

Davison, C. (2019). Using assessment to enhance learning in English language education. In X. Gao (Ed.), *Second handbook of English language teaching*. Springer International Handbooks of Education. Springer. https://doi.org/10.1007/978-3-030-02899-2_21

Demirci, C., & Düzenli, H. (2017). Formative value of an active learning strategy: technology-based think-pair-share in an EFL writing classroom. *World Journal of Education*, *7*(6), 63-74. https://doi.org/10.5430/wje.v7n6p63

Engle, M. (2017). *How to prepare an annotated bibliography: the annotated bibliography*. Cornell University Library. https://guides.library.cornell.edu/annotatedbibliography

Erdogan, T., & Yurdabakan, I. (2011). Secondary school students' opinions on portfolio assessment in EFL. *International Journal on New Trends in Education and Their Implications*, *2*(3), 63-72.

Estaji, M., & Fassihi, S. (2016). On the relationship between the implementation of formative assessment strategies and Iranian EFL teachers' self-efficacy: do gender and experience make a difference? *Journal of English Language Teaching and Learning*, *8*(18), 65-86. https://elt.tabrizu.ac.ir/article_5494.html

Fakeye, D. O. (2016). Secondary school teachers' and students' attitudes towards formative assessment and corrective feedback in English language in Ibadan Metropolis. *Journal of Educational and Social Research*, *6*(2), 141-148. https://doi.org/10.5901/jesr.2016.v6n2p141

Gan, Z., & Leung, C. (2020). Illustrating formative assessment in task-based language teaching. *ELT Journal, 74*(1), 10-19. https://doi.org/10.1093/ELT/CCZ048

Gattullo, F. (2000). Formative assessment in ELT primary (elementary) classrooms: an Italian case study. *Language Testing, 17*(2), 278-288. https://doi.org/10.1177/026553220001700210

Graham, S., Harris, K. R., & Hebert, M. A. (2011). *Informing writing: the benefits of formative assessment. A Carnegie Corporation Time to Act Report.* Alliance for Excellence in Education. https://www.carnegie.org/publications/informing-writing-the-benefits-of-formative-assessment/

Guadu, Z. B., & Boersma, E. J. (2018). EFL instructors' beliefs and practices of formative assessment in teaching writing. *Journal of Language Teaching and Research, 9*(1), 42-50. https://doi.org/10.17507/jltr.0901.06

Haines, K., Meima, E., & Faber, M. (2013). Formative assessment and the support of lecturers in the international university. In *International Experiences in Language Testing and Assessment* (pp. 177-190). Peter Lang.

Hansson, S. (2015). *Benefits and difficulties in using peer response for writing in the EFL classroom.* Göteborgs Universitet. https://gupea.ub.gu.se/bitstream/2077/38436/1/gupea_2077_38436_1.pdf

Harner, J. L. (2000). On compiling an annotated bibliography. *Modern Language Association of America.*

Hattie, J., & Timperley, H. (2007). The power of feedback. *Review of Educational Research, 77*(1), 81-112.

Heritage, M. (2019). Feedback for enhanced English language learning. In X. Gao (Ed.), *Second handbook of English language teaching* (pp. 497-515). Springer International Handbooks of Education. Springer. https://doi.org/10.1007/978-3-030-02899-2_27

Heritage, M., & Chang, S. (2012). Teacher use of formative assessment data for English language learners. *National Centre for Research on Evaluation, Standards, & Student Testing.* https://cresst.org/wp-content/uploads/ELL_Symposium_FINAL.pdf

Herrera, L., & Macías, D. F. (2015). A call for language assessment literacy in the education and development of teachers of English as a foreign language. *Colombian Applied Linguistics Journal, 17*(2), 302-312. https://doi.org/10.14483/udistrital.jour.calj.2015.2.a09

Huang, S. C. (2012). Like a bell responding to a striker: instruction contingent on assessment. *English Teaching: Practice and Critique, 11*(4), 99-119. https://files.eric.ed.gov/fulltext/EJ999757.pdf

Huang, S. C. (2016). No longer a teacher monologue – involving EFL writing learners in teachers' assessment and feedback processes. *Taiwan Journal of TESOL, 13*(1), 1-31. http://www.tjtesol.org/attachments/article/402/04_TJTESOL-273.pdf

Hyland, F. (2000). ESL writers and feedback: giving more autonomy to students. *Language Teaching Research, 4*(1), 33-54.

Jian, H., & Luo, S. (2014). Formative assessment in L2 classroom in China: the current situation, predicament and future. *Indonesian Journal of Applied Linguistics, 3*(2), 18-34. https://doi.org/10.17509/ijal.v3i2.266

Jiang, Y. (2014). Exploring teacher questioning as a formative assessment strategy. *RELC Journal, 45*(3), 287-304. https://doi.org/10.1177/0033688214546962

Joo, S. H. (2016). Self and peer assessment of speaking. *Studies in Applied Linguistics and TESOL, 16*(2). https://doi.org/10.7916/salt.v16i2.1257

Joyce, P. (2018). The effectiveness of online and paper-based formative assessment in the Learning of English as a second language. *PASAA, 5,* 126-146. https://www.culi.chula.ac.th/publicationsonline/files/article/W8Mo0m4nyBMon110741.pdf

Karagianni, E. (2012). Employing computer assisted assessment (CAA) to facilitate formative assessment in the State Secondary School: a case study. *Research Papers in Language Teaching and Learning, 3*(1), 252-268. http://rpltl.eap.gr/images/2012/03-01-252-Karagianni.pdf

Ketabi, S., & Ketabi, S. (2014). Classroom and formative assessment in second/foreign language teaching and learning. *Theory & Practice in Language Studies, 4*(2), 435-440. https://doi.org/10.4304/tpls.4.2.435-440

Kızıl, V., & Yumru, H. (2019). The impact of self-assessment: a case study on a tertiary level EFL writing class. *Mevzu – Sosyal Bilimler Dergisi, 1,* 35-54. https://dergipark.org.tr/en/pub/mevzu/issue/44858/517475

Kuo, C. L. (2015). *A quasi-experimental study of formative peer assessment in an EFL writing classroom.* Unpublished doctoral dissertation. Newcastle University. http://theses.ncl.ac.uk/jspui/handle/10443/2863

Lam, R. (2015). Language assessment training in Hong Kong: implications for language assessment literacy. *Language Testing, 32*(2), 169-197. https://doi.org/10.1177/0265532214554321

Lam, R. (2018). Understanding assessment as learning in writing classrooms: the case of portfolio assessment. *Iranian Journal of Language Teaching Research, 6*(3), 19-36. https://doi.org/10.30466/ijltr.2018.120599

Lazzeri, S., Cabezas, X., Ojeda, L., & Leiva, F. (2015). Automated formative evaluations for reading comprehension in an English as a foreign language course: benefits on performance, user satisfaction, and monitoring of higher education students in Chile. In F. Helm, L. Bradley, M. Guarda & S. Thouësny (Eds), *CriticalCALL – proceedings of the 2015 EUROCALL Conference*, Padova, Italy (pp. 355-361). Research-publishing.net. https://doi.org/10.14705/rpnet.2015.000358

Leung, C., & Rea-Dickins, P. (2007). Teacher assessment as policy instrument: contradictions and capacities. *Language Assessment Quarterly, 4*(1), 6-36. https://doi.org/10.1080/15434300701348318

Levy, T., & Gertler, H. (2015). Harnessing technology to assess oral communication in Business English. *Teaching English with Technology, 15*(4), 52-59. https://files.eric.ed.gov/fulltext/EJ1138436.pdf

Little, D. (2002). The European Language Portfolio: structure, origins, implementation and challenges. *Language Teaching, 35*(3), 182-189. https://doi.org/10.1017/S0261444802001805

Meissner, M. C. (2018). *Formative assessment at the intersection of principles, practice and perceptions*. Master's thesis. Faculty of Education and Natural Sciences, Inland Norway University of Applied Sciences. https://brage.inn.no/inn-xmlui/bitstream/handle/11250/2560247/Meissner.pdf?sequence=1

Memorial University Libraries. (n.d.). *How to evaluate information resources*. https://www.library.mun.ca/researchtools/guides/doingresearch/evaluateall/

Muñoz, A. P., Palacio, M., & Escobar, L. (2012). Teachers' beliefs about assessment in an EFL context in Colombia. *Profile Issues in Teachers Professional Development, 14*(1), 143-158.

Naghdipour, B. (2017). Incorporating formative assessment in Iranian EFL writing: a case study. *The Curriculum Journal, 28*(2), 283-299. https://doi.org/10.1080/09585176.2016.1206479

Oakley, A. (2012). Foreword. In D. Gough, S. Oliver & J. Thomas (Eds), *An introduction to systematic reviews* (pp. vii-x). Sage Publications.

Öz, H. (2014). Turkish teachers' practices of assessment for learning in the English as a foreign language classroom. *Journal of Language Teaching & Research, 5*(4). https://doi.org/10.4304/jltr.5.4.775-785

Papadima-Sophocleous, S. (2017). L2 assessment and testing teacher education: an exploration of alternative assessment approaches using new technologies. In K. Borthwick, L. Bradley & S. Thouësny (Eds), *CALL in a climate of change: adapting to turbulent global conditions – short papers from EUROCALL 2017* (pp. 248-253). Research-publishing.net. https://doi.org/10.14705/rpnet.2017.eurocall2017.721

Phung, H. V. (2016). Portfolio assessment in second/foreign language pedagogy. *Hawaii Pacific University TESOL Working Paper Series 14*, 90-107. https://www.hpu.edu/research-publications/tesol-working-papers/2016/07HuyPhung.pdf

Pinto-Llorente, A. M., Sánchez-Gómez, M. C., García-Peñalvo, F. J., & Martín, S. C. (2016, November). The use of online quizzes for continuous assessment and self-assessment of second-language learners. In *Proceedings of the Fourth International Conference on Technological Ecosystems for Enhancing Multiculturality* (pp. 819-824). https://doi.org/10.1145/3012430.3012612

Poehner, M. E., & Lantolf, J. P. (2005). Dynamic assessment in the language classroom. *Language Teaching Research, 9*(3), 233-265. https://doi.org/10.1191/1362168805lr166oa

Ponce, H. R., Mayer, R. E., Figueroa, V. A., & López, M. J. (2018). Interactive highlighting for just-in-time formative assessment during whole-class instruction: effects on vocabulary learning and reading comprehension. *Interactive Learning Environments, 26*(1), 42-60. https://doi.org/10.1080/10494820.2017.1282878

Radford, B. W. (2014). *The effect of formative assessments on languageperformance*. Unpublished doctoral dissertation. Brigham Young, Provo. http://scholarsarchive.byu.edu/etd/3978

Ranalli, J., Link, S., & Chukharev-Hudilainen, E. (2017). Automated writing evaluation for formative assessment of second language writing: investigating the accuracy and usefulness of feedback as part of argument-based validation. *Educational Psychology, 37*(1), 8-25. https://doi.org/10.1080/01443410.2015.1136407

Rea-Dickins, P. (2004). Understanding teachers as agents of assessment. *Language Testing, 21*(3), 249-258. https://doi.org/10.1191/0265532204lt283ed

Rea-Dickins, P., & Gardner, S. (2000). Snares and silver bullets: disentangling the construct of formative assessment. *Language Testing, 17*(2), 215-243. https://doi.org/10.1177/026553220001700206

Restrepo, A., & Nelson, H. (2013). Role of systematic formative assessment on students' views of their learning. *Profile Issues in Teachers Professional Development, 15*(2), 165-183. http://www.scielo.org.co/scielo.php?pid=S1657-07902013000200011&script=sci_arttext&tlng=pt

Rezaee, A. A., Alavi, S. M., & Shabani, E. A. (2013). Alternative assessment or traditional testing: how do Iranian EFL teachers respond? *Teaching English Language, 7*(2), 151-190. https://doi.org/10.22132/TEL.2013.54864

Saglam, A. L. G. (2018). The integration of educational technology for classroom-based formative assessment to empower teaching and learning. In A. Khan & S. Umair (Eds), *Handbook of research on mobile devices and smart gadgets in K-12 rducation* (pp. 321-341). IGI Global. https://doi.org/10.4018/978-1-5225-2706-0.ch020

Saito, H., & Inoi, S. I. (2017). Junior and senior high school EFL teachers' use of formative assessment: a mixed-methods study. *Language Assessment Quarterly, 14*(3), 213-233. https://doi.org/10.1080/15434303.2017.1351975

Saliu Abdulahi, D. (2017). Scaffolding writing development: how formative is the feedback? *Moderna språk, 111*(1), 127-155. https://www.duo.uio.no/handle/10852/59613

Saliu Abdulahi, D., Hellekjær, G. O., & Hertzberg, F. (2017). Teachers' (formative) feedback practices in EFL writing classes in Norway. *Journal of Response to Writing, 3*(1), 31-55. https://journalrw.org/index.php/jrw/article/view/69

Sardareh, S. (2018). Formative feedback in a Malaysian primary school ESL context. *MOJES: Malaysian Online Journal of Educational Sciences, 4*(1), 1-8. https://mojes.um.edu.my/article/view/12640

Seyyedrezaie, Z. S., Ghansoli, B., Shahriari, H., & Fatemi, A. H. (2016). Examining the effects of Google docs-based instruction and peer feedback types (implicit vs. explicit) on EFL learners' writing performance. *CALL-EJ, 17*(1), 35-51. http://callej.org/journal/17-1/Seyyedrezaie_Ghonsooly_Shahriari_Fatemi2016.pdf

Shin, S. Y. (2013). Developing a framework for using e-portfolios as a research and assessment tool. *ReCALL, 25*(3), 359-372. https://doi.org/10.1017/S0958344013000189

Shore, J. R., Wolf, M. K., & Heritage, M. (2016). A case study of formative assessment to support teaching of reading comprehension for English learners. *Journal of Educational Research & Innovation, 5*(2), 1-19. https://digscholarship.unco.edu/jeri/vol5/iss2/4

Şişman, E. P., & Büyükkarci, K. (2019). A review of foreign language teachers' assessment literacy. *Sakarya University Journal of Education, 9*(3), 628-650. https://doi.org/10.19126/suje.621319

Smith, D. H., & Davis J. E. (2014). Formative assessment for student progress and programme improvement in sign language as L2 programmes. In D. McKee, R. S. Rosen & R. McKee (Eds), *Teaching and learning signed languages* (pp. 253-280). Palgrave Macmillan. https://doi.org/10.1057/9781137312495_12

Stabler-Havener, M. L. (2018). Defining, conceptualising, problematising, and assessing language teacher assessment literacy. *Studies in Applied Linguistics and TESOL, 18*(1). https://doi.org/10.7916/salt.v18i1.1195

Stiggins, R. J. (2007). Conquering the formative assessment frontier. In J. McMillian (Ed.), *Formative classroom assessment* (pp. 8-28). Columbia University Teachers College Press.

Tabatabaei, O., & Assefi, F. (2012). The effect of portfolio assessment technique on writing performance of EFL learners. *English Language Teaching, 5*(5), 138-147. https://doi.org/10.5539/elt.v5n5p138

Tang, J., Rich, C. S., & Wang, Y. (2012). Technology-enhanced English language writing assessment in the classroom. *Chinese Journal of Applied Linguistics, 35*(4), 385-399.

Tang, L. (2016). Formative assessment in oral English classroom and alleviation of speaking apprehension. *Theory and Practice in Language Studies, 6*(4), 751-756. https://doi.org/10.17507/tpls.0604.12

Tavakoli, E., Amirian, S. M. R., Burner, T., Davoudi, M., & Ghaniabadi, S. (2018). Operationalization of formative assessment in writing: an intuitive approach to the development of an instrument. *Applied Research on English Language, 7*(3), 319-344. https://doi.org/10.22108/ARE.2018.112373.1340

Tavakoli, E., Amirian, M. R., Burner, T., Davoudi, M., & Ghaniabadi, S. (2019). Formative assessment of writing (FAoW): a confirmatory factor structure study. *International Journal of Assessment Tools in Education, 6*(3), 344-361. https://doi.org/10.21449/ijate.544277

The Writing Center, University of Colorado Denver | Anschutz Medical Campus. (2014). Annotated bibliography https://clas.ucdenver.edu/writing-center/sites/default/files/attached-files/annotated_bibliographies.pdf

Titova, S. (2015). Use of mobile testing system PeLe for developing language skills. In F. Helm, L. Bradley, M. Guarda & S. Thouësny (Eds), *Critical CALL – proceedings of the 2015 EUROCALL Conference* (pp. 523-528). Research-publishing.net. https://doi.org/10.14705/rpnet.2015.000387

Tsagari, D. (2004). Is there life beyond language testing? An introduction to alternative language assessment. *CRILE Working Papers, 58*, 1-23. https://pdfs.semanticscholar.org/19ad/ddb4879992814f8ebbc323a8d6f2dd491a4f.pdf

Tsagari, D. (2016). Assessment orientations of state primary EFL teachers in two Mediterranean countries. *Center for Educational Policy Studies Journal, 6*(1), 9-30. https://doi.org/10.26529/cepsj.102

Tsagari, D., & Michaeloudes, G. (2013). Formative assessment patterns in CLIL primary schools in Cyprus. In S. Ioannou-Georgiou, S. Papadima-Sophocleous & D. Tsagari (Eds), *International experiences in language testing and assessment* (pp. 75-93). Peter Lang Edition.

Tuttle, H. G., & Tuttle, A. (2013). *Improving foreign language speaking through formative assessment*. Routledge. https://doi.org/10.4324/9781315854854

UNSW Sydney Current Students. (n.d.). Annotated bibliography. https://www.student.unsw.edu.au/annotated-bibliography

Vågen, M. T. (2017). *Formative assessment in EFL writing: a case study of pupils' perceptions of their feedback practice and attitudes to receiving and using feedback*. Master's thesis. University of Bergen.

Vassiliou, S., & Papadima-Sophocleous, S. (2019). A systematic review and annotated bibliography of second language learning formative assessment: an overview. *Conference Proceedings, 12th International Conference Innovation in Language Learning* (pp. 352-362). https://conference.pixel-online.net/ICT4LL/files/ict4ll/ed0012/Conference%20Proceedings.pdf

Wang, X. (2017). A Chinese EFL teacher's classroom assessment practices. *Language Assessment Quarterly*, *14*(4), 312-327. https://doi.org/10.1080/15434303.2017.1393819

Widiastuti, I. A. M. S., Mukminatien, N., Prayogo, J. A., & Irawati, E. (2020). Dissonances between teachers' beliefs and practices of formative assessment in EFL classes. *International Journal of Instruction*, *13*(1), 71-84. https://doi.org/10.29333/iji.2020.1315a

Widiastuti, I. A. M. S., & Saukah, A. (2017). Formative assessment in EFL classroom practices. *Bahasa dan Seni: Jurnal Bahasa, Sastra, Seni, dan Pengajarannya*, *45*(1), 50-63. https://doi.org/10.17977/um015v45i12017p050

Williamson, K., & Sadera, E. (2016). Electronic formative feedback and its effect on the writing skills of Asian L2 postgraduate students. *DEANZ2016: Conference Proceedings* (pp. 208-210). https://kiwibelma.files.wordpress.com/2016/05/deanz16-conference-proceedings11-april.pdf

Wolf, M. K., Shore, J. R., & Blood, I. (2014). *English learner formative assessment (ELFA): a design framework*. ETS. https://www.ets.org/s/research/pdf/elfa_design_framework.pdf

Xie, Q., & Lei, Y. (2019). Formative assessment in primary English writing classes: a case study from Hong Kong. *The Asian EFL Journal*, *23*(5), 55-95.

Yarahmadzehi, N., & Goodarzi, M. (2020). Investigating the role of formative mobile-based assessment in vocabulary learning of pre-intermediate EFL learners in comparison with paper-based assessment. *Turkish Online Journal of Distance Education*, *21*(1), 181-196.

Zhao, H. (2014). Investigating teacher-supported peer assessment for EFL writing. *ELT Journal*, *68*(2), 155-168. https://doi.org/10.1093/elt/cct068

Conclusions

According to the literature, most research publications in the long history of L2 assessment mainly focus on Summative Assessment (SA), e.g. on testing, high stakes examinations, and the various aspects related to them, such as validity, reliability, washback, and impact. Attention has only been shed on Formative Assessment (FA) in the last 20 years. More research in this area would prove beneficial, not only to researchers, but to undergraduate and postgraduate students, language practitioners, policymakers, and other stakeholders. By the same token, an overview of what has been researched in FA in the last 20 years and extensive knowledge of this domain would be equally useful.

This book contributes to the literature on the work of language formative assessment that has been published from 2000 to 2020, an area which is relatively new and requires further investigation. The authors' intention was to fill the gaps of the non-existence of Systematic Review (SR) and Annotated Bibliography (AB) in the area of FA in Language Learning (LL). As part of this, we examined the research conducted so far on FA and we established that the definition of FA is not completed yet, it is in its making. For this reason, although we established the main characteristics of FA discussed so far by different researchers, it was not our intention to explore, when the authors of the sources we examined, mentioned they practised FA in LL, or whether their claim actually had characteristics of FA. Our aim was to record both in the SR and the AB the activity in the area of FA in LL, based on our FA definition.

Furthermore, the present book records the history of L2FA in two ways, where one complements the other: in the form of an SR and in the form of a descriptive and evaluative AB, from the very first published work on the subject in 2000 to the end of 2020. The SR presents an overview of different aspects of FA in a chronological order. It gives insights into information such as the types

Conclusions

of language FA of the research publications; the research purposes; the type of research designs; the research tools and methods used in the studies; the research purposes; the languages which the publications researched; the type of participants involved in the studies; the level of educational institutions the research was carried out in; the types of FA applications in LL; the language focus; the learning theories and teaching methods used to support the specific language FA; the geographic distribution of these studies; the types of technology and their use in LL FA; the necessity of training for both the students and the teachers; and other features such as anxiety, etc. The data is synthesised and conclusions are reached regarding the profile of the research published during the period under study. The AB consists of bibliographical citations and entries that have been placed in chronological order from 2000 to 2020, and included 104 annotations. Each annotation describes and evaluates the content of each entry.

Based on the SR and the AB, further research could explore the nature of FA in the sources included here and inspire more investigations in light of new circumstances and needs in the field of language education.

www.ingramcontent.com/pod-product-compliance
Lightning Source LLC
Chambersburg PA
CBHW031630160426
43196CB00006B/351